Our selection of the city's best [places to] eat, drink and experience:

◉ **Sights**

✪ **Eating**

🚇 **Drinking**

✪ **Entertainment**

🔒 **Shopping**

These symbols give you the vital information for each listing:

| | |
|---|---|
| ☏ Telephone Numbers | 👪 Family-Friendly |
| ⌚ Opening Hours | 🐾 Pet-Friendly |
| P Parking | 🚌 Bus |
| 🚭 Nonsmoking | ⛴ Ferry |
| @ Internet Access | 🚊 Tram |
| 🛜 Wi-Fi Access | 🚆 Train |
| 🍴 Vegetarian Selection | |
| 🍽 English-Language Menu | |

Find each listing quickly on maps for each neighbourhood:

**Bar Hemingway**

16 🚇 Map p233, B2

Legend has it that Hemi self, wielding a machine [li]berate this timber-pan[elled] [cov]ered bar during [WWII. The] showpiece is a [cognac give]n by Papa ar [anywhere in] town. Dress [...s.com; Hôtel Rit] ⌚6.30pm-2a[m]

6 ◉ Plac[e] V[...]

are designed to get you straight to the heart of the city.

Inside you'll find all the must-see sights, plus tips to make your visit to each one really memorable. We've split the city into easy-to-navigate neighbourhoods and provided clear maps so you'll find your way around with ease. Our expert authors have searched out the best of the city: walks, food, nightlife and shopping, to name a few. Because you want to explore, our 'Local Life' pages will take you to some of the most exciting areas to experience the real Sydney.

And of course you'll find all the practical tips you need for a smooth trip: itineraries for short visits, how to get around, and how much to tip the guy who serves you a drink at the end of a long day's exploration.

It's your guarantee of a really great experience.

## Our Promise

You can trust our travel information because Lonely Planet authors visit the places we write about, each and every edition. We never accept freebies for positive coverage, so you can rely on us to tell it like it is.

# QuickStart Guide 7

# Explore Sydney 21

## Worth a Trip:

## Pocket
# SYDNEY

**TOP SIGHTS • LOCAL LIFE • MADE EASY**

# In This Book

## QuickStart Guide

Your keys to understanding the city – we help you decide what to do and how to do it

**Need to Know**
Tips for a smooth trip

**Neighbourhoods**
What's where

## Explore Sydney

The best things to see and do, neighbourhood by neighbourhood

**Top Sights**
Make the most of your visit

**Local Life**
The insider's city

## The Best of Sydney

The city's highlights in handy lists to help you plan

**Best Walks**
See the city on foot

**Sydney' Best...**
The best experiences

## Survival Guide

Tips and tricks for a seamless, hassle-free city experience

**Getting Around**
Travel like a local

**Essential Information**
Including where to stay

# QuickStart Guide

## Welcome to Sydney

Canberra may be the capital, but Sydney is Australia's first city. The nation's birthplace, it's exuberant, sassy and stacks of fun. Brash and shallow? Whatever... Sydney's sunny self-confidence is reinforced by its famously picturesque harbour and numerous beautiful beaches. And if it's ever feeling blasé about its natural assets, a dizzying whirl of shopping, dining and partying carries on regardless.

Sydney Harbour, including Sydney Harbour Bridge (p28) and Sydney Opera House (p24, designed by architect Jørn Utzon)
PHILLIP HAYSON / CORBIS ©

# Sydney Top Sights

### Sydney Opera House (p24)

Striking, unique, curvalicious – is there a sexier building on the planet? What goes on inside (opera, theatre, dance, concerts) is almost as interesting as the famous exterior.

### Bondi Beach (p124)

A quintessential Sydney experience, Bondi Beach offers munificent opportunities for lazing on the sand, languishing in bars and cafes, carving up the surf, splashing about in the shallows and swimming in sheltered pools.

### Royal Botanic Gardens (p26)

Although the bustle of the city couldn't be closer, these spacious gardens are superbly tranquil – the only conspicuous traffic is the purposeful procession of ferries on the harbour.

### Art Gallery of NSW (p46)

The stately neoclassical building that houses the Art Gallery of NSW doesn't divulge the exuberance of the collection it contains. Step inside and enter a world of creativity in the John Kaldor Family Gallery. *Full artwork credits on p191.*

### Taronga Zoo (p42)

Even if every single one of Taronga Zoo's 4000 or so animals was hiding or on vacation, the ferry ride and harbour views would still make for a fantastic day out.

RICHARD I'ANSON / GETTY IMAGES ©

GREG ELMS/ / GETTY IMAGES ©

### Sydney Harbour Bridge (p28)

Like the Opera House, Sydney's second most loved construction inhabits the intersection of practicality and great beauty. The harbour views it provides are magnificent.

## Sydney Aquarium (p66)

Well laid out and absolutely fascinating, this large complex has an impressive array of gigantic sharks and rays. Don't miss a rare opportunity to get up close and personal with a dugong.

ANDREW HOLT / ALAMY ©

AFP/ GETTY IMAGES ©

## Australian Museum (p96)

Historical collections of minerals and bones compete with 'dangerous Australians' and dinosaurs in this grande dame of Sydney museums. The Aboriginal section is particularly interesting.

# Sydney Local Life

*Insider tips to help you find the real city*

After checking out the tourist sights, take some time to see what the locals are up to – on the river, on the fringes of the harbour, and in the city's financial, political, educational and fashion districts.

## A Journey up Parramatta River (p40)

▶ River life
▶ Industrial sites

Circular Quay may seem like the heart of the city, but Sydney's geographical centre is actually 20km upstream in Parramatta. A ferry ride west displays a different side of the city, revealing historical working-class neighbourhoods and the remnants of riverside industry.

## Meandering along Macquarie St (p48)

▶ Convict architecture
▶ Civic institutions

Macquarie St was the civic showcase of the early convict colony and it is no less so today.

It's here that the state's politicians continue their age-old squabbles over water and transport.

## Studying the University of Sydney (p78)

▶ Museums
▶ Student hang-outs

The large campus of Sydney Uni dominates the suburbs on the city's western flank. While its Hogwartsian stone walls may suggest primness and properness, that's quite far from the reality of Sydney student life.

## A Saturday in Paddington (p110)

▶ Markets
▶ Cafes & bars

Paddington revels in its reputation as the city's fashion and art quarter, and although its boutiques may be struggling to compete with nearby megamalls, its leafy streets still offer plenty of neighbourhood charm.

## Wandering Around Woolloomooloo (p114)

▶ Historic wharf
▶ Backstreet pubs

Woolloomooloo's rough-edged reputation has taken a beating in recent years. Once known for its sozzled seadogs, tough-as-nails dockworkers and randy marines, the Finger Wharf is now full of movie-star apartments, luxurious hotel rooms

OLIVER STREWE / GETTY IMAGES ©

Paddington (p110)

Watson's Bay (p134)

and top-dollar restaurants. Thankfully the beer and pies remain.

## A Day in Watsons Bay (p134)

▶ Beaches
▶ Views

This once remote fishing village has some of Sydney's best harbour beaches and most dramatic clifftop views. Ogle the city's priciest harbourside real estate on the ferry ride, then stake your claim to one of the neighbourhood's hidden beaches.

MISHKACZ / DREAMSTIME.COM ©

### Other great places and ways to experience the city like a local:

Yum cha in Chinatown (p55)

Live music at Inner West pubs (p87)

Darlinghurst's gay scene (p105)

Sydney Fish Market (p72)

Surfing in Manly (p141)

Barracking for the Sea Eagles in a Manly pub (p143)

Chippendale (p82)

# Sydney Day Planner

## Day One

☀ Start at Circular Quay and head directly to the **Sydney Opera House** (p24). Circle around it and follow the shoreline into the **Royal Botanic Gardens** (p26). Have a good look about and then continue around **Mrs Macquaries Point** (p27) and down to Woolloomooloo. Grab a pie at **Harry's Cafe de Wheels** (p114), a Sydney institution.

☀ Head back up to the **Art Gallery of NSW** (p46). Take some time to explore the gallery then cross **The Domain** (p54) and cut through **Sydney Hospital** (p49) to Macquarie St. **Parliament House** (p49) is immediately to the right, while to the left is the **Mint** (p49) and **Hyde Park Barracks** (p48). Cross into **Hyde Park** (p52) and head straight through its centre, crossing Park St and continuing on to the **Anzac Memorial** (p52).

☾ Catch a cab to **Porteño** (p102) in Surry Hills. After dinner, if you haven't booked tickets for a play at **Belvoir St Theatre** (p106) or a gig at the **Gaelic Club** (p108), take a stroll along Crown St. There are plenty of good bars and pubs to stop at along the way.

## Day Two

☀ Catch the bus to **Bondi Beach** (p124) and spend some time swimming, strolling about and soaking it all in. Once you're done, take the clifftop path to **Tamarama Beach** (p128) and on to **Bronte** (p128), where you can grab lunch at **Three Blue Ducks** (p130).

☀ Continue on the coastal path through **Waverley Cemetery** (p128) and down to **Clovelly Beach** (p128). This is a great spot to stop for a swim or a snorkel. Continuing on you'll pass Gordons Bay and Dolphin Point before you arrive at **Coogee Beach** (p128). Stop for a drink in the beer garden of the **Coogee Bay Hotel** (p132) then jump onboard a bus back to Bondi Junction, where you can switch to the train network.

☾ Everyone needs at least one trashy night up the Cross. Start with cocktails at **Jimmy Liks** (p121) before dinner at **Fratelli Paradiso** (p118). Top it off afterwards with a tipple at **Gazebo Wine Garden** (p120). Then **Sugarmill** (p121), **Kings Cross Hotel** (p120), **World Bar** (p121)...

**Short on time?**

We've arranged Sydney's must-sees into these day-by-day itineraries to make sure you see the very best of the city in the time you have available.

## Day Three

☀ Take the scenic ferry ride from Circular Quay to Watsons Bay. Walk up to **The Gap** (p135) to watch the waves pounding against the cliffs, then continue on to **Camp Cove** (p135) for a dip. Take the **South Head Heritage Trail** (p135) for sublime views of the city and the whole of the upper harbour. For lunch, pull up a pew with a view at the **Watsons Bay Hotel** (p135).

☀ Head back to Circular Quay and spend the afternoon exploring The Rocks. Start at the **Museum of Contemporary Art** (p32) and then head up to **The Rocks Discovery Museum** (p32). Continue through the Argyle Cut to Millers Point and wander up **Observatory Hill** (p32). Double back under the **Sydney Harbour Bridge** (p28).

☾ If last night was your trashy night, make this your glamorous one. Book ahead for one of the upmarket Circular Quay restaurants and a show at the **Sydney Opera House** (p24). Finish up at **Opera Bar** (p36) or one of the old pubs in The Rocks, such as the **Lord Nelson** (p36) or **Hero of Waterloo** (p36).

## Day Four

☀ Have a stroll around the waterfront and settle on whichever of the big attractions takes your fancy – perhaps the **Australian National Maritime Museum** (p69), **Sydney Aquarium** (p66) or **Wild Life Sydney** (p71). Each of these will easily fill up an entire morning. For a quick bite, pop up to **Central Baking Depot** (p56).

☀ Jump on the river service at King St Wharf and take an hour-long cruise upstream as far as **Sydney Olympic Park** (p41). Take a stroll along the river until the next ferry arrives to whisk you back. Stop off on **Cockatoo Island** (p41) for a look at its art installations and the remnants of its convict and shipbuilding past. From here you can either catch a ferry to Balmain, or head straight back to Darling Harbour or Circular Quay.

☾ After dinner at **Bloodwood** (p84) stroll along King St in Newtown and cruise the late-night bookstores and bars.

# Need to Know

**For more information,
see Survival Guide (p167)**

### Currency
Australian dollar ($)

### Language
English

### Visas
The only visitors who do not require a visa in advance of arriving in Australia are New Zealanders.

### Money
There are ATMs everywhere and major credit cards are widely accepted.

### Mobile Phones
New Zealand and European phones will accept local SIM cards. Quad-band North American handsets will work but need to be unlocked to accept a SIM.

### Time
Eastern Standard Time (GMT/UTC plus 10 hours)

### Plugs & Adaptors
Standard voltage is 220 to 240 volts AC (50Hz). Plugs are flat three-pin types, with the top two pins angled.

### Tipping
If the service is good, it is customary to tip at restaurants (up to 10%) and in taxis (round up to the nearest dollar).

## ① Before You Go

### Your Daily Budget

#### Budget less than $190
▶ Dorm beds $23–48
▶ Hanging out at the beach or free sights
▶ Free hostel breakfasts, with burgers or cheap noodles for lunch and dinner, all up $15

#### Midrange $190–320
▶ Private room with own bathroom $100–220
▶ Cafe breakfast and lunch $15 each
▶ Two-course dinner with glass of wine $45

#### Top End more than $320
▶ Four-star hotel from $220
▶ Three-course dinner with wine in top restaurant $120–200
▶ Opera ticket $150
▶ Taxis $50

#### Useful Websites
▶ **Destination NSW** (www.sydney.com) Official visitors' guide.

**City of Sydney** (www.cityofsydney.nsw.gov.au) Visitor information, disabled access and parking.

▶ **Sydney Morning Herald** (www.smh.com .au) News and events.

▶ **Time Out** (www.au.timeout.com/sydney) Reviews and events.

▶ **Lonely Planet** (www.lonelyplanet.com /sydney) Traveller forum.

#### Advance Planning

**Three months prior** Book accommodation; make sure your passport and visa are in order.

**One month prior** Book top restaurants and a show at the Opera House.

**A week prior** Check the Sydney news websites.

# 2 Arriving in Sydney

The vast majority of visitors to Sydney arrive at Sydney airport (SYD; www.sydneyairport .com.au), also known as Kingsford Smith airport, 10km south of the city centre. Long-distance trains chug into Sydney's Central station.

## ✈ From Sydney Airport

| Destination | Best Transport |
| --- | --- |
| Circular Quay & The Rocks | Sydney Airporter Shuttle |
| City Centre | Sydney Airporter Shuttle |
| Newtown | Taxi |
| Bondi | Taxi |
| Manly | Manly Express Shuttle |

## ✈ At the Airport

**Sydney Airport** The airport has separate international (T1) and domestic (T2 and T3) terminals, 4km apart on either side of the runway. Each terminal has eateries, left-luggage services, ATMs, currency exchange bureaux and rental car counters. The international terminal offers plenty of opportunity for duty-free shopping.

# 3 Getting Around

Visitors should find Sydney's public transport easy to use and reasonably efficient. If you're here for a week, a MyMulti1 pass will get you most places you'd want to go on trains, ferries, buses and trams. Otherwise buy off-peak return tickets.

## 🚆 Train

Generally the best way to get around, with reliable and reasonably frequent central services.

## 🚌 Bus

Buses will get you to all the places that trains don't go, such as the Eastern Beaches and Vaucluse.

## 🚊 Light Rail

Connects Central station, Pyrmont and Glebe, but nowhere else you're likely to go.

## ⛴ Ferry

An excellent way to see the harbour and the best option for getting from the city to Manly, Watsons Bay, Taronga Zoo, Cockatoo Island and Balmain.

## 🚗 Car

Handy for getting to the beaches, but a liability around the central city due to hefty parking charges.

## 🚕 Taxi

Reasonably priced for short trips around central neighbourhoods.

## ⛴ Water Taxi

Expensive but quick and flexible way of getting around the harbour.

# Sydney Neighbourhoods

**Worth a Trip**
**⊙ Top Sights**
Taronga Zoo

**Circular Quay & The Rocks (p22)**
The historic heart of Sydney, containing its most famous sights.
**⊙ Top Sights**
Sydney Opera House
Royal Botanic Gardens
Sydney Harbour Bridge

**City Centre & Haymarket (p44)**
Sydney's central business district offers plenty of choices for shopping, eating and sightseeing, with colonial buildings scattered among the skyscrapers.
**⊙ Top Sights**
Art Gallery of NSW

**Darling Harbour & Pyrmont (p64)**
Unashamedly tourist focused, Darling Harbour tempts visitors to its shoreline bars and restaurants with fireworks displays and a sprinkling of glitz.
**⊙ Top Sights**
Sydney Aquarium

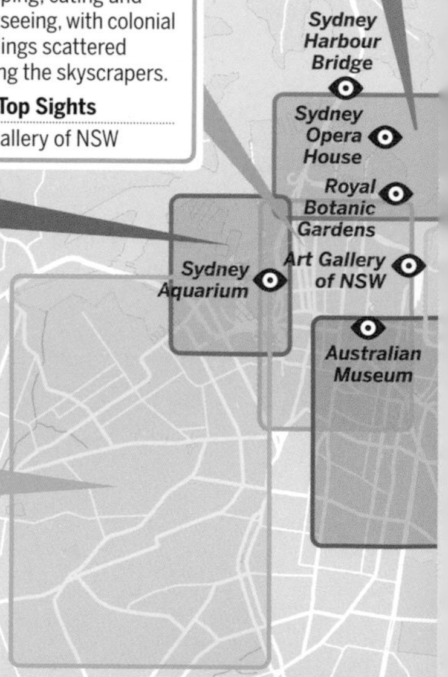

**Inner West (p76)**
Quietly bohemian Glebe and more loudly bohemian Newtown are the most well known of the Inner West's tightly packed suburbs, grouped around the University of Sydney.

*Sydney Harbour Bridge* ⊙

*Sydney Opera House* ⊙

*Royal Botanic Gardens* ⊙

*Sydney Aquarium* ⊙

*Art Gallery of NSW* ⊙

⊙ *Australian Museum*

**Kings Cross & Potts Point (p112)**
Strip joints, tacky tourist shops and backpacker hostels bang heads with classy restaurants, funky bars and gorgeous guesthouses as 'the Cross' pumps 24/7.

**Manly (p136)**
The only place in Sydney where you can catch a ferry to swim in the ocean, Manly caps off the harbour with scrappy charm.

**Surry Hills & Darlinghurst (p94)**
Home to a mishmash of inner-city hipsters, yuppies, a large gay and lesbian community, and an array of excellent bars and eateries.

👁 **Top Sights**
Australian Museum

**Bondi to Coogee (p122)**
Improbably good-looking arcs of sand framed by jagged cliffs, the Eastern Beaches are a big part of the Sydney experience.

👁 **Top Sights**
Bondi Beach

**Bondi Beach**

# Explore
# **Sydney**

## Worth a Trip

Sydney Opera House (p24), designed by architect Jørn Utzon
GLENN VAN DER KNIJFF / GETTY IMAGES ©

Explore

# Circular Quay &
# The Rocks

The birthplace of both the city and the nation, this compact area seamlessly combines the historic with the exuberantly modern. Circular Quay's promenade serves as a backdrop for buskers of mixed merit and locals disgorging from harbour ferries. Join the tourist pilgrimage to the Opera House and Harbour Bridge, then grab a pint at a convict-era pub in The Rocks.

# The Sights in a Day

Why postpone joy? Start at Circular Quay and head directly to the **Sydney Opera House** (p24). Follow the shoreline into the **Royal Botanic Gardens** (p26), then continue to **Mrs Macquaries Point** (p27). When you've seen enough, backtrack to Circular Quay and call into the **Customs House** (p32). Continue around to Circular Quay West and pop up to **Sailors Thai Canteen** (p36) for lunch.

Spend the afternoon exploring The Rocks. Start at the **Museum of Contemporary Art** (p32) and then head up into the network of narrow lanes to **The Rocks Discovery Museum** (p32) and **Susannah Place Museum** (p32). Continue through the Argyle Cut to Millers Point and wander up the hill to **Sydney Observatory** (p32). Pop into one of Sydney's oldest pubs, perhaps the **Lord Nelson Brewery Hotel** (p36), and then cut down to Walsh Bay and double back under the **Sydney Harbour Bridge** (p28).

Book well in advance for Sydney's top restaurant, **Quay** (p34), followed by a show at the Sydney Opera House or Walsh Bay. Otherwise head to **Opera Bar** (p36) to be mesmerised by the lights sparkling on the water.

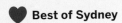

## Top Sights

Sydney Opera House (p24)

Royal Botanic Gardens (p26)

Sydney Harbour Bridge (p28)

## Best of Sydney

**Eating**

Quay (p34)

**Bars & Pubs**

Opera Bar (p36)

Hero of Waterloo (p36)

Lord Nelson Brewery Hotel (p36)

Blu Bar on 36 (p37)

**Historic Buildings**

Susannah Place (p32)

## Getting There

**Train** Circular Quay is one of the City Circle stations.

**Ferry** Circular Quay is Sydney's ferry hub and has services to Watsons Bay, Manly, Taronga Zoo, Darling Harbour, Cockatoo Island and Balmain, among others.

**Bus** Several bus routes terminate at Circular Quay, including services to/from Glebe, Newtown, Surry Hills, Darlinghurst, Kings Cross, Paddington, Bondi, Coogee and Watsons Bay.

## Top Sights
# Sydney Opera House

Gazing upon the Sydney Opera House with virgin eyes is a sure way to send a tingle down your spine. Danish architect Jørn Utzon's competition-winning 1956 design is Australia's most recognisable visual image. Gloriously white, curvaceous and pointy, it perches dramatically at the tip of Bennelong Point, waiting for its close-up. No matter which angle you point a lens at it, it shamelessly mugs for the camera; it really doesn't have a bad side.

◉ Map p30, E2

☏ 9250 7111

www.sydneyoperahouse
.com

Bennelong Point

🚊 Circular Quay

Sydney Opera House

# Don't Miss

### Exterior

The House's dramatic shape is thought to have been inspired by billowing sails. It's not until you get close that you realise that the seemingly solid expanse of white is actually composed of tiles; 1,056,000 self-cleaning, cream-coloured, Swedish tiles to be exact.

### Performances

Dance, concerts, opera and theatre are staged in the Concert Hall, Opera Theatre, Drama Theatre and Playhouse, while more intimate and left-of-centre shows inhabit the Studio. The acoustics in the Concert Hall are superb. Companies that regularly perform here include Opera Australia, Sydney Theatre Company, Bangarra Dance Theatre and the Australian Ballet.

### Tours

The interiors don't live up to the promise of the dazzling exterior, but if you're curious to see inside, one-hour **guided tours** (⏸9250 7777; adult/child/family $35/25/90; ⏱9am-5pm) depart half-hourly. For a more in-depth look, the two-hour early-morning **backstage tour** (tickets $155; ⏱7am) includes the Green Room and dressing rooms.

### Utzon Room

The interior of this room is the only one to have been designed by the great man himself, before he quit the project in disgust in 1966. Construction of the House started in 1959 but after a tumultuous clash of egos, delays, politicking and cost blowouts, the Opera House finally opened in 1973. Utzon and his son Jan were commissioned for renovations in 2004, but Utzon died in 2008 having never seen his finished masterpiece in the flesh.

## ☑ Top Tips

▸ Most performances (2400 of them annually) sell out quickly, but partial view tickets are often available on short notice.

▸ The free monthly *What's On* brochure lists upcoming events.

▸ You'll save $5 on tours if you book online.

▸ Not all tours can visit all theatres because of rehearsals, but you're more likely to see everything if you go early.

▸ Kids at the House is a pint-sized entertainment roster of music, drama and dance.

## ✗ Take a Break

Call into Opera Bar (p36) on the lower concourse on the Circular Quay side of the Opera House for an alfresco beverage and dazzling harbour views.

Set within the Opera House's smallest sail, Guillaume at Bennelong (p35) is one of the city's top restaurants.

## Top Sights
# Royal Botanic Gardens

These expansive gardens are the inner city's favourite picnic destination, jogging route and snuggling spot for loved-up couples. Bordering Farm Cove, east of the Sydney Opera House, the gardens were established in 1816 and feature plant life from Australia and around the world. They include the site of the colony's first paltry vegetable patch, but their history goes back much further than that; long before the convicts arrived this was an initiation ground for the Cadigal people.

Map p30, F4

9231 8111

www.rbgsyd.nsw.gov.au

Mrs Macquaries Rd

admission free

7am–sunset

Circular Quay

Royal Botanic Gardens

# Don't Miss

## Government House

Encased in English-style grounds within the gardens, **Government House** (☏9931 5222; www.hht.net.au; Macquarie St; admission free; ⊙grounds 10am-4pm, tours 10.30am-3pm Fri-Sun; ☒Circular Quay) is a Gothic sandstone mansion which served as the home of NSW's governors from 1846 to 1996. The governor still uses it for weekly meetings and hosting visiting heads of state and royalty. Unless there's a bigwig in town, you can tour through.

## Sydney Tropical Centre

The **Sydney Tropical Centre** (☏9231 8104; adult/child/family $5.50/3.30/11; ⊙10am-4pm) comprises the interconnecting Arc and Pyramid glasshouses. The Arc has a rampant collection of climbers from the world's rainforests; the Pyramid houses Australian species.

## Mrs Macquaries Point

Adjoining the gardens, Mrs Macquaries Point forms the northeastern tip of Farm Cove and provides beautiful views over the bay to the Opera House and city skyline. It was named in 1810 after Elizabeth, Governor Macquarie's wife, who ordered a seat chiselled into the rock from which she could view the harbour.

## Tours

Free 1½-hour guided walks depart at 10.30am daily from the information booth outside the Gardens Shop. From March to November there's also an additional hour-long tour at 1pm on weekdays. Book ahead for an **Aboriginal Heritage Tour** (☏9231 8134; adult/child $33/17; ⊙10am Fri), which covers local history, traditional plant uses and bush-food tastings. You can also download self-guided tours from the RBG website.

## ☑ Top Tips

▶ If you're all walked out, take a ride on the **Choochoo Express** (www.choochoo.com.au; adult/child $10/5; ⊙11am-4pm), a trackless train that departs from Queen Elizabeth II Gate (nearest the Opera House) every half hour.

▶ The park's paths are mostly wheelchair accessible.

## ✕ Take a Break

The **Botanic Gardens Restaurant & Cafe** (Map p30, F5; www.trippas whitegroup.com.au; mains $29-32; ⊙breakfast Sat & Sun, lunch daily) is situated within rainforest near the centre of the park.

Back on Circular Quay, Matt Moran's Aria (p36) offers white-linen weekday lunches.

## Top Sights
# Sydney Harbour Bridge

Whether they're driving over it, climbing up it, jogging across it, shooting fireworks off it or sailing under it, Sydneysiders adore their bridge and swarm around it like ants on ice cream. Dubbed the 'coathanger', it's a spookily big object – moving around town you'll catch sight of it in the corner of your eye, sometimes in the most surprising of places. Perhaps Sydney poet Kenneth Slessor said it best: 'Day and night, the bridge trembles and echoes like a living thing.'

 Map p30, C1

🚊 Circular Quay

BridgeClimb, Sydney Harbour Bridge

# Don't Miss

## The Structure

At 134m high, 502m long, 49m wide and weighing 53,000 tonnes, the Sydney Harbour Bridge is the largest and heaviest (but not the longest) steel arch in the world. The two halves were built outwards from each shore and were finally bolted together in 1932 after nine years' construction by 1400 workers. Stairs access the bridge from both shores and a footpath runs along its eastern side.

## Pylon Lookout

The bridge's hefty pylons may look as though they're shouldering all the weight, but they're largely decorative – right down to their granite facing. There are awesome views from the top of the **Pylon Lookout** (☎9240 1100; www.pylonlookout .com.au; adult/child $11/6.50; ⊙10am-5pm), atop the southeast pylon, 200 steps above the bridge's footpath. Inside the pylon there are exhibits explaining how the bridge was built.

## BridgeClimb

Once only painters and daredevils scaled the Harbour Bridge. Now, thanks to **BridgeClimb** (☎8274 7777; www.bridgeclimb.com; 3 Cumberland St; adult $188-298, child $128-198), anyone can do it (Bruce Springsteen, Bette Midler, Will Smith...). The scariest part is crossing over the grates while under the bridge; on the curved span itself the track is wide enough that you never see straight down. Tours last 2¼ to 3½ hours.

## ☑ Top Tips

▶ The best way to experience the bridge is on foot – don't expect much of a view crossing by train or car.

▶ A pre-BridgeClimb toilet stop is a smart idea.

▶ The priciest climbs are at dawn and twilight.

▶ The bridge is the centrepiece of Sydney's major celebrations, particularly the New Year's Eve fireworks.

## ✗ Take a Break

Call into the Harbour View Hotel (p37) for a post-bridge beverage.

At the northern end, **Ripples** (☎9929 7722; www.ripplesmilsonspoint .com.au; Olympic Dr, Milsons Point; breakfast $12-18, lunch & dinner $29-32; ⊙breakfast, lunch & dinner; ⛴Milsons Point/Luna Park) serves reliable seafood dishes combining the flavours of Asia and Europe.

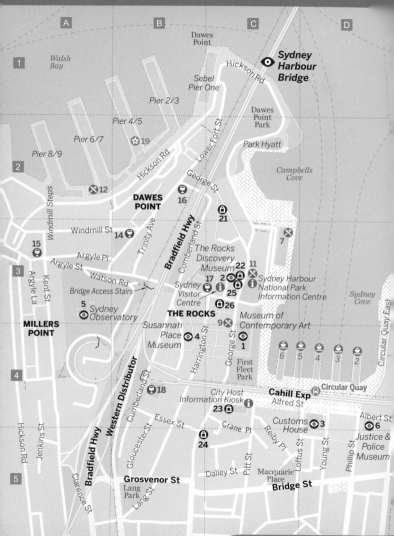

**30** Circular Quay & The Rocks

Walsh Bay

Dawes Point

Sydney Harbour Bridge

Hickson Rd

Sebel Pier One

Pier 2/3

Pier 4/5

☆ 19

Pier 6/7

Pier 8/9

Dawes Point Park

Park Hyatt

Campbells Cove

✕ 12

DAWES POINT

Windmill Steps

Hickson Rd

George St

Lower Fort St

16

21

Windmill St

14

15

Argyle Pl

Argyle St

Watson Rd

Bridge Access Stairs

Trinity Ave

Bradfield Hwy

Cumberland St

7

The Rocks Discovery Museum

22  11

17  2

Sydney Harbour National Park Information Centre

25

Sydney Visitor Centre

26

THE ROCKS

5  Sydney Observatory

MILLERS POINT

Kent St

Argyle La

Susannah Place Museum

4

9

Museum of Contemporary Art

1

Harrington St

George St

First Fleet Park

Sydney Cove

Circular Quay East

6  5  4  3  2

18

Cumberland St

Western Distributor

Bradfield Hwy

Gloucester St

Essex St

Crane Pl

City Host Information Kiosk

23

Alfred St

Cahill Exp

Circular Quay

Customs House

3

Reiby Pl

Albert St

6

Justice & Police Museum

24

Dalley St

Pitt St

Macquarie Place

Loftus St

Young St

Phillip St

Grosvenor St

Lang Park

Lang St

Clarence St

Hickson Rd

Jenkins St

Bridge St

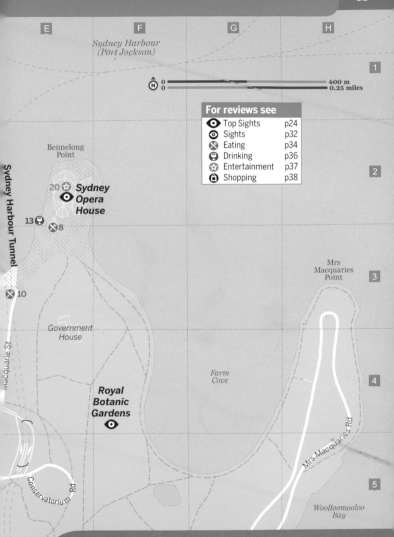

E   F   G   H

*Sydney Harbour*
*(Port Jackson)*

1

N   0                                    400 m
    0                                    0.25 miles

**For reviews see**
- ⊙ Top Sights        p24
- ⊙ Sights            p32
- ✕ Eating            p34
- ☕ Drinking          p36
- ★ Entertainment     p37
- 🔒 Shopping          p38

Bennelong
Point

2

20 ★  **Sydney**
⊙   *Opera*
    *House*

13 ⊟
✕8

Sydney Harbour Tunnel

Mrs
Macquaries
Point

3

✕10

*Government*
*House*

Macquarie St

**Royal
Botanic
Gardens**
⊙

*Farm
Cove*

Mrs Macquaries Rd

4

5

*Conservatorium Rd*

*Woolloomooloo
Bay*

# Sights

## Museum of Contemporary Art
GALLERY

1 ⊙ Map p30, C4

A slice of Gotham City on Circular Quay West, the MCA has been raising even the most open-minded Sydney eyebrows since 1991. Constantly changing exhibitions range from the incredibly hip to in-your-face, sexually explicit and profoundly disturbing. You'll also find Aboriginal art featured prominently. Quite simply, it's one of Australia's best and most challenging galleries. (MCA; ☏9245 2400; www.mca.com.au; 140 George St; admission free; ☉10am-5pm Fri-Wed, 10am-9pm Thu; ⊠Circular Quay)

## The Rocks Discovery Museum
MUSEUM

2 ⊙ Map p30, C3

Divided into four chronological displays – Warrane (pre-1788), Colony (1788–1820), Port (1820–1900) and Transformations (1900 to the present), this excellent museum digs deep into The Rocks' history and leads you on an artefact-rich tour. Sensitive attention is given to The Rocks' original inhabitants, the Cadigal people. (☏9240 8680; www.rocksdiscoverymuseum.com; Kendall La; admission free; ☉10am-5pm; ⊠Circular Quay)

## Customs House
HISTORIC BUILDING

3 ⊙ Map p30, D4

This gracious harbourside edifice (1885) houses the three-level **Customs House Library** (☏9242 8555; ☉10am-7pm Mon-Fri, 11am-4pm Sat & Sun), with a great selection of international newspapers and magazines, internet access and interesting temporary exhibitions. In the lobby, look for the swastikas in the tiling and a charmingly geeky 1:500 model of the inner city under the glass floor. (☏9242 8551; www.sydney customshouse.com.au; 31 Alfred St; admission free; ☉8am-midnight Mon-Fri, 10am-midnight Sat, 11am-5pm Sun; ⊠Circular Quay)

## Susannah Place Museum
MUSEUM

4 ⊙ Map p30, B4

Dating from 1844, Susannah Place is a diminutive terrace of tiny houses with a tiny shop selling tiny historical wares. My, haven't we grown? In the backyard, check out how generations of working class Rocks women cooked and laundered their clothes in a wood-fired copper urn (near the outdoor dunny). Admission is by way of guided tour. (☏9241 1893; www.hht.net.au; 58-64 Gloucester St; adult/child/family $8/4/17; ☉2-6pm Mon-Fri, 10am-6pm Sat, Sun & school holidays; ⊠Circular Quay)

## Sydney Observatory
OBSERVATORY

5 ⊙ Map p30, A3

Built in the 1850s, Sydney's copper-domed, Italianate observatory squats atop **Observatory Hill**, overlooking

## Understand

## Colonial Beginnings

When the American War of Independence disrupted the transportation of convicts to North America, Britain lost its main dumping ground for undesirables and needed somewhere else to put them. Joseph Banks, who had been Lieutenant James Cook's scientific leader during the expedition in 1770, piped up with the suggestion that Botany Bay would be a fine new site for criminals.

### First Fleet

The 11 ships of the First Fleet landed at Botany Bay in January 1788 – a motley crew of 730 male and female convicts, 400 sailors, four companies of marines, and enough livestock and booze to last two years. Captain Arthur Phillip quickly rejected Botany Bay as a suitable site for a settlement and sailed 25km north to the harbour Cook had named Port Jackson, where he discovered a crucial source of fresh water in what he called Sydney Cove (today's Circular Quay). The day was 26 January 1788, now celebrated as Australia Day. Conversely, many Aborigines refer to it as 'Invasion Day' or 'Survival Day'.

### The Disreputable Rocks

The socio-economic divide of the future city was foreshadowed when the convicts were allocated the rocky land to the west of the stream (known unimaginatively as The Rocks), while the governor and other officials pitched their tents to the east.

Built with convict labour between 1837 and 1844, Circular Quay was originally (and more accurately) called Semi-circular Quay, and acted as the main port of Sydney. In the 1850s it was extended further, covering over the, by then, festering Tank Stream which ran through the middle.

As time went on, whalers and sailors joined the ex-convicts at The Rocks – and inns and brothels sprang up to entertain them. With the settlement filthy and overcrowded, the nouveau riche started building houses on the upper slopes, their sewage flowing to the slums below. Bubonic plague broke out in 1900, leading to the razing of entire streets, while the Harbour Bridge's construction in the 1920s wiped out even more. It wasn't until the 1970s that The Rocks' cultural and architectural heritage was finally recognised.

Millers Point and the harbour. Inside is a collection of vintage apparatus, including Australia's oldest working telescope (1874). Also on offer are audiovisual displays, a virtual-reality **3D Space Theatre** (adult/child/family $8/2/22; ⊗2.30pm & 3.30pm daily, plus 11am & noon Sat & Sun) and an interactive Australian astronomy exhibition including Aboriginal sky stories and modern stargazing. (☑9921 3485; www.sydneyobservatory.com.au; Watson Rd; admission free; ⊗10am-5pm; ◉Circular Quay)

### Justice & Police Museum

MUSEUM

 Map p30, D4

In the old Water Police Station (1858), this mildly unnerving museum mimics a late-19th-century police station and court. Focusing on disreputable activities, exhibits include weapons, butt-ugly mugshots, forensic evidence from Sydney's most heinous crimes and at least two stuffed dogs. Wheelchair access to the ground floor only. (☑9252 1144; www.hht.net.au; cnr Albert & Phillip Sts; adult/child/family $10/5/20; ⊗9.30am-5pm; ◉Circular Quay)

# Eating

## Quay

MODERN AUSTRALIAN $$$

7  Map p30, C3

Quay is shamelessly guilty of breaking the rule that good views make for bad food. Peter Gilmore may be one of Sydney's younger celeb chefs, but Quay's exquisite menu proves he's at the top of his game. And the view? Like dining in a postcard – as long as there's not a cruise ship in the way. Bookings essential. (☑9251 5600;

---

### Understand
#### Bennelong

Bennelong was born around 1764 into the Wangal tribe, who lived around Glebe. In 1789 he was kidnapped on the orders of Governor Arthur Phillip, who hoped to use the captive to learn the customs and language of the reclusive locals. Eventually he escaped, but returned by 1791 when reassured that he would not be held against his will. He learnt to speak English and developed a friendship with Governor Phillip, who had a brick hut built for him on what is now Bennelong Point, where the Sydney Opera House stands.

In 1792, Bennelong went on a 'civilising' trip to England, and returned in 1795 with a changed dress sense and altered behaviour. Described as good-natured and 'stoutly made', Bennelong ultimately was no longer accepted by Aboriginal society and never really found happiness with the colonists either. He died a broken, dispossessed man in 1813, possibly as a result of his affection for the bottle.

SUSAN SEUBERT / CORBIS ©

Guillaume at Bennelong

www.quay.com.au; L3, Overseas Passenger Terminal; set menu lunch/dinner $125/165; ☺lunch Tue-Fri, dinner daily; ◫Circular Quay)

### Guillaume at Bennelong
FRENCH $$$

8  Map p30, E3

Turn the old 'dinner and a show' cliché into something meaningful under the smallest sail at the Sydney Opera House. Snuggle into a banquette and enjoy the masterful cuisine of acclaimed chef Guillaume Brahimi. His contemporary French fare has fans hollering operatically all over town. Book well ahead. (☎9241 1999; www.guillaumeatbennelong.com.au; Sydney Opera House; 2 courses $95; ☺lunch Thu & Fri, dinner Tue-Sat; ◫Circular Quay)

### Rockpool
MODERN AUSTRALIAN $$$

9  Map p30, C3

The Neil Perry empire now stretches to seven acclaimed restaurants in three cities but it was here, in the dying days of the 1980s, that it all began. After two decades, the original Rockpool's creations still manage to wow the critics – expect crafty, contemporary cuisine with Asian influences, faultless service and an alluring wine list. (☎9252 1888; www.rockpool.com; 107 George St; 2 courses $100; ☺lunch Fri & Sat, dinner Tue-Sat; ◫Circular Quay)

### Aria
MODERN AUSTRALIAN **$$$**

10  Map p30, E3

Aria is a star in Sydney's fine-dining firmament, an award-winning combination of chef Matt Moran's stellar dishes, awesome Sydney Opera House views and faultless service. Pre- and after-theatre supper menus are available. Reservations essential. (☏9252 2555; www.ariarestaurant.com; 1 Macquarie St; mains $48; ⏱lunch Mon-Fri, dinner daily; ☒Circular Quay)

### Sailors Thai Canteen
THAI **$$**

11  Map p30, C3

Wedge yourself into a gap between arts-community operators, politicians and media manoeuvrers at Sailors' long communal table and order from the fragrant menu of Thai street food classics. The balcony tables fill up fast, but fortune might be smiling on you. Downstairs at the restaurant, the vibe's more formal and the prices higher. (☏9251 2466; www.sailorsthai.com.au; 106 George St; mains $17-29; ⏱lunch & dinner; ☒Circular Quay)

### Firefly
TAPAS **$$**

12  Map p30, A2

Compact, classy and never snooty, Firefly's outdoor candlelit tables fill with pre-theatre patrons having a quick meal before the show (Sydney Theatre is across the road). Come after 8pm when the audience has taken its seats, and tuck into some grilled haloumi, *piquillo* pepper croquettes and fine wine. Great cocktails, too. (☏9241 2031; www.fireflybar.com.au; Pier 7, 17 Hickson Rd; tapas $14-19; ⏱11am-11pm Mon-Sat; ☒Wynyard)

# Drinking

### Opera Bar
BAR, LIVE MUSIC

13  Map p30, E2

The Opera Bar puts all other beer gardens to shame. Right on the harbour with the Opera House on one side and the Harbour Bridge on the other, this perfectly positioned terrace manages a very Sydney marriage of the laid-back and the sophisticated. There's live music from 8.30pm weekdays and from 2pm on weekends. (www.operabar.com.au; lower concourse, Sydney Opera House; ⏱11.30am-midnight Sun-Thu, to 1am Fri & Sat; ☒Circular Quay)

### Hero of Waterloo
PUB, LIVE MUSIC

14  Map p30, B3

Enter this rough-hewn 1843 sandstone pub to meet some locals, chat-up the Irish bar staff and grab an earful of the swing, folk, bluegrass and Celtic bands (Friday to Sunday). Downstairs is an original dungeon where drinkers would sleep off a heavy night before being shanghaied to the high seas via a tunnel leading straight to the harbour. (☏9252 4553; www.heroofwaterloo.com.au; 81 Lower Fort St; ⏱9.30am-11.30pm Mon-Sat, noon-10pm Sun; ☒Circular Quay)

### Lord Nelson Brewery Hotel
PUB, BREWERY

**15**  Map p30, A3

Built in 1836 and converted into a pub in 1841, the 'Nello' claims to be Sydney's oldest pub (although a couple of other pubs dispute that). The on-site brewery cooks up robust stouts and ales (try the Old Admiral Ale), and there's decent midrange accommodation upstairs if you've had a few too many. (☑9251 4044; www.lordnelson.com.au; 19 Kent St; ☺11am-11pm Mon-Sat, noon-10pm Sun; ☒Circular Quay)

### Harbour View Hotel
PUB

**16**  Map p30, B2

Built in the 1920s, the curvilicious Harbour View was the main boozer for the Harbour Bridge construction crew. These days it fulfils the same duties for the BridgeClimbers – wave to them from the 2nd-floor balcony as they traverse the lofty girders. The Tooth's KB Lager listed on the tiles out the front is long gone, but there's plenty of Heineken and Boag's on tap. (☑9252 4111; www.harbourview.com.au; 18 Lower Fort St; ☺11am-midnight Mon-Sat, to 10pm Sun; ☒Circular Quay)

### Argyle
BARS, DJ

**17**  Map p30, C3

This mammoth conglomeration of five bars is spread through the historic sandstone Argyle Stores buildings, with everything from a cobblestone courtyard to underground cellars resonating with DJs. The decor ranges from rococo couches to white extruded plastic tables, all offset with kooky chandeliers and moody lighting. Great bar food, too. (☑9247 5500; www.theargylerocks.com; 18 Argyle St; ☒Circular Quay)

### Blu Bar on 36
COCKTAIL BAR

**18**  Map p30, B4

The drinks may be pricey but it's well worth heading up to this bar at the top of the Shangri-La hotel for the views, which seem to stretch all the way to New Zealand. The dress code is officially 'smart casual' but err on the side of smart if you can't handle rejection. (☑9250 6000; www.shangri-la.com; L36, 176 Cumberland St; ☺5pm-midnight Mon-Thu, 5pm-1am Fri & Sat, 5-11pm Sun; ☒Circular Quay)

## Entertainment

### Sydney Theatre Company
THEATRE

**19**  Map p30, B2

Established in 1978, the STC is Sydney theatre's top dog and has been an important stepping stone in the careers of many famous Australian actors. Hour-long tours of the company's Wharf and Sydney theatres are held at 10.30am on the first and third Thursdays of the month ($10). Performances are also staged at the Sydney Opera House's Drama Theatre. (STC; ☑9250 1777; www.sydneytheatre.com.au; Pier 4/5,

## Understand
## Performing Arts

With the Opera House as its centrepiece, it follows that this neighbourhood is the locus of Sydney's performing arts scene. Walsh Bay, on the other side of The Rocks, is home to four major companies and two excellent theatre complexes. If you're keen to spot famous thespians, there are few better locales.

15 Hickson Rd; tickets free-$90; ⊙box office 9am-7pm Mon, to 8.30pm Tue-Fri, 11am-8.30pm Sat, 2hr before show Sun; ℝWynyard)

## Opera Australia                    OPERA

 Map p30, E2

Opera Australia is the big player in Oz opera, staging more than 600 performances a year. The company is based both in the Sydney Opera House and in Melbourne. (☑9318 8200; www.opera-australia.org.au; Sydney Opera House; tickets $85-297; ℝCircular Quay)

## Bangarra Dance Theatre    DANCE

Bangarra (see 19 ⭐ Map p30, B2) is hailed as Australia's finest Aboriginal performance company. Artistic director Stephen Page conjures a fusion of contemporary themes and indigenous traditions, blending Torres Strait Islander dance with Western technique. It often performs at the Sydney Opera House, as well as interstate and internationally. (☑9251 5333; www.bangarra.com.au; Pier 4/5, 15 Hickson Rd; tickets $33-196; ℝWynyard)

## Sydney Dance Company    DANCE

Australia's number one contemporary dance company has been lubricating the nation's cultural psyche for more than 25 years, staging wildly modern, sexy, sometimes shocking works. SDC dance lessons are just $20. Performances are usually held across the street at Sydney Theatre (see 19 ⭐ Map p30, B2). (SDC; ☑9221 4811; www.sydneydancecompany.com; Pier 4/5, 15 Hickson Rd; tickets $30-99; ℝCircular Quay)

## Australian Ballet                DANCE

The Melbourne-based Australian Ballet performs a wide repertoire of classic as well as contemporary works. See them twinkle their toes at the Opera House. (☑1300 369 741; www.australianballet.com.au; tickets $33-176)

## Sydney Symphony    CLASSICAL MUSIC

The Sydney Symphony is blessed with principal conductor and artistic director Vladimir Ashkenazy and plays 140 concerts annually with famous local and international musicians. Catch them at the Sydney Opera House and City Recital Hall. (☑02 8215 4600; www.sydneysymphony.com; tickets $35-159)

# Shopping

## The Rocks Market
MARKET

**21** 🔒 Map p30, C2

Under a long white canopy, the 150 stalls at the weekend market are a little on the tacky side of the tracks (opals, faux Aboriginal art etc) but are still worth a gander. The Friday 'Foodies Market' is more fulfilling (and filling). (www.therocksmarket.com; George St; ⏱10am-4pm Fri-Sun; 🚉Circular Quay)

## Puppet Shop at The Rocks
TOYS

**22** 🔒 Map p30, C3

Puppet master Phillip (all the way from the Belgian Congo) beguiles you with his accent as you 'enter the dazzling caves of wonders'. Dangling from the ceiling of his sandstone cellar are hundreds of incredible handmade wizards, skeletons, soldiers, jesters and spooky Chinese puppets. We'd hate to come here at night... (📞9247 9137; www.thepuppetshop.com; 77 George St; ⏱10am-5pm; 🚉Circular Quay)

## Australian Wine Centre
WINE

**23** 🔒 Map p30, C4

This basement store with multilingual staff is packed with quality Australian wine, beer and spirits. Pick up some Hunter Valley semillon or organise a shipment back home. Healthy wallets can access Cuban cigars and a staggering range of prestigious Penfolds Grange wines. (📞9247 2755; www.australianwinecentre.com; Goldfields House, 1 Alfred St; 🚉Circular Quay)

## Opal Fields
JEWELLERY

**24** 🔒 Map p30, B5

Billing itself as 'the world's largest opal retailer', this family firm has been turning out jewellery designs incorporating Australia's most famous gemstone for more than 30 years. There's another store at 388 George St. (📞9247 6800; www.opalfields.com.au; 190 George St; 🚉St James)

## Original & Authentic Aboriginal Art
ART

**25** 🔒 Map p30, C3

This trustworthy gallery specialises in works from the Central and Western Deserts, Arnhem Land, the Kimberley, Queensland, New South Wales and Victoria. There is information available on the artists, and some more unusual work for sale, such as painted glass and traditional sand paintings preserved on canvas. (📞9251 4222; www.authaboriginalart.com.au; 79 George St; 🚉Circular Quay)

## Gannon House
ART

**26** 🔒 Map p30, C3

Specialising in contemporary Australian and Aboriginal art, Gannon House purchases works directly from artists and Aboriginal communities. You'll find the work of prominent artists such as Gloria Petyarre here, alongside lesser-known names. (📞9251 4474; www.gannonhousegallery.com; 45 Argyle St; 🚉Circular Quay)

## Local Life
# A Journey up the Parramatta River

### Getting There

🛳 Catch the ferry from Circular Quay to Balmain East (Darling St). The cheapest option for the day is to buy a MyMulti DayPass ($21).

Sydney Harbour gets all the attention but a jaunt upriver is just as interesting and provides an opportunity to stop and explore along the way. As you pass old industrial sites and gaze into millionaires' backyards, a window opens onto a watery world in the heart of Sydney where school rowing crews get put through their paces, groups of mates glide past on yachts and solo kayakers work up a sweat.

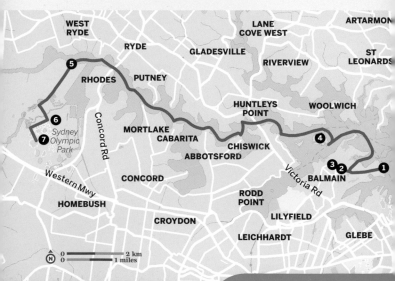

## ❶ Wander through Balmain

Once a tough, working-class neighbourhood, Balmain is home to dozens of historically significant buildings. As you head up Darling St look for **Waterman's Cottage** (1841) at No 12; **Cathermore** (1841), Balmain's first bakery, which later became the Waterford Arms pub, at No 50; and the **Watch House** (1854), Sydney's oldest surviving lock-up, at No 179.

## ❷ Adriano Zumbo Patisserie

Australia's highest profile pastry chef introduced the nation to macarons during a stint on TV's *MasterChef*. Call into his **patisserie** (296 Darling St; $3-18; ☺8am-6pm; 🚢Balmain) to stock up on 'Zumbarons', tarts and cakes as astonishing to look at as they are to eat.

## ❸ Rock the Kazbah

Balmain's best restaurant, **Kazbah** (📞9555 7067; www.kazbah.com.au; 379 Darling St; breakfast $15-22, lunch $21-26, dinner $31-38; ☺breakfast & lunch Tue-Sun, dinner Tue-Sat; 🚢Balmain West) is an Aladdin's cave filled with Moorish decorations and the flavours of the Maghreb. On hot summer days the windows fold out and the locals pour in for brunch.

## ❹ Explore Cockatoo Island

Catch a ferry from Balmain (Thames St) to fascinating Cockatoo Island, positioned where the harbour and river meet. A spooky tunnel passes clear through the island and you can explore the remains of a convict-era prison and shipyard.

## ❺ Cycle Sydney Olympic Park

Continue by ferry to 640-hectare Sydney Olympic Park. More than just Olympic nostalgia, it incorporates nature reserves and 35km of cycleways. The best way to explore is by **bike** (www.bikehiresydneyolympicpark.com.au); on weekends and school holidays you can also hire them from Blaxland Riverside Park, 1.5km west along the river from the ferry wharf.

## ❻ Take the Brickpit Ring Walk

This brightly coloured circular **walkway** (Australia Ave; ☺sunrise-sunset), an Olympic Park attraction, sits 18m above an abandoned brickworks on what looks like metal chopsticks. Three billion bricks were made here between 1911 and 1988. Built into the loop are multimedia exhibits about the brick workers and their amphibious replacements, including the endangered green and golden bell frog.

## ❼ Check out ANZ Stadium

The main Olympic venues are 3km from the wharf, so you're best to cycle or catch bus 526. **ANZ Stadium** (📞8765 2300; www.anzstadium.com.au; Olympic Blvd; tours adult/child $29/19; ☺tours 11am, 1pm & 3pm; 🚃Olympic Park), the main arena, is an imposing oval bedpan with a colourful sculpture of native feathers spiralling over its entrance. The **Sydney Olympic Park Visitor Centre** (📞9714 7888; www.sydney olympicpark.com.au; 1 Showground Rd; ☺9am-5pm; 🚃Olympic Park) and the Olympic Park train station are nearby.

# Top Sights
## Taronga Zoo

### Getting There

Taronga Zoo is located in Mosman on the North Shore, roughly halfway between Circular Quay and Manly.

🚢 The best way to get there is by ferry from Circular Quay.

A day trip to Taronga offers so much more than the zoo itself: running the gauntlet of didgeridoo players and living statues at Circular Quay; the ferry ride past the Opera House and out into the harbour; the cable car from the wharf to the top gate; the ever-present views of the city skyline as you make your way down through 75 hectares of bushy harbour hillside. And to cap it all off, the enclosures are excellent, too.

Taronga Zoo

# Don't Miss

### Australian Natives

As you'd expect, Taronga Zoo is chock-full of kangaroos, koalas and similarly hirsute Australian creatures. The zoo's 4000 critters have million-dollar harbour views but seem blissfully unaware of the privilege. The animals are well looked after, with more natural open enclosures than cages. Highlights include the nocturnal platypus habitat and the Great Southern Oceans section.

### Talks & Encounters

Throughout the day there are keeper-led feedings, educational talks and demonstrations. One of the highlights is the bird show at midday and 3pm, where remarkably tame raptors and parrots swoop over an open-air amphitheatre facing the harbour. Equally popular is the seal show, featuring Australian and Californian sea lions and New Zealand fur seals.

### Tours

Tours include **Nura Diya** (☎9978 4782; 90-minute tour adult/child $99/69; ⏱9.45am Mon, Wed & Fri), where indigenous guides introduce you to native animals and share Dreamtime stories about them, while giving an insight into traditional Aboriginal life. The **Wild Australia Experience** (adult/child $124/78; ⏱10am & 2pm) is a small group tour with a keeper that allows entry into the koala enclosure, the opportunity to hand-feed kangaroos and wallabies, and behind-the-scenes access to the Nightlife house.

### Roar & Snore Sleepover

The overnight **Roar & Snore** (☎9978 4791; adult/child $275/190) experience includes a night-time safari, a buffet dinner, breakfast and tents under the stars.

---

☎9969 2777

www.taronga.org.au

Bradleys Head Rd

adult/child $44/22

⏱9am-5pm, last admission 4.30pm

🚢Taronga Zoo

## ☑ Top Tips

▶ A **Zoo Pass** (adult/child/family $51/25/143) from Circular Quay includes return ferry rides, the bus or cable car ride to the top and zoo admission.

▶ Parking is scarce – take public transport instead.

▶ Disabled access is good, even if arriving by ferry, and wheelchairs are available.

## ✗ Take a Break

**Cafe Harbourview** (mains $11-16; ⏱10am-4pm) is the zoo's main eatery. There's another cafe in the top plaza entrance, and kiosks, takeaways and picnic areas are scattered about the grounds.

Explore

# City Centre & Haymarket

Before suburban sprawl started in earnest in the mid-19th century, this area (along with The Rocks) *was* Sydney. Today it's a towering central business district (CBD) – Australia's economic engine room – with skyscrapers shadowing sandstone colonial buildings and churches. The breathless jumble of Haymarket and Chinatown provides the yin to the CBD's yang.

## The Sights in a Day

Spend most of the morning exploring the **Art Gallery of NSW** (p46), then stroll through **The Domain** (p54) to **St Mary's Cathedral** (p52). Cross into **Hyde Park** (p52) and head straight through its centre, crossing Park St and continuing on to the **Anzac Memorial** (p52). Pop down to Chinatown for lunch; **Mamak** (p56) is an excellent option.

Explore **Chinatown** (p52): wander through Dixon St and into **Paddy's Markets** (p63). Head back along George St to the **Town Hall** (p54) and **Queen Victoria Building** (p62). If the shopping bug bites, continue on to Sydney's main shopping strip, Pitt St Mall, in the shadow of **Sydney Tower** (p53); **Westfield Sydney** (p62), **Myer** (p63), **David Jones** (p63) and the **Strand Arcade** (p62) are all here. Once you're all shopped out, spend the rest of your afternoon at the **Museum of Sydney** (p53).

Head to **Chat Thai** (p56) for a bite before seeking out some of the city's petite, tucked-away bars: **Grandma's** (p59), **Baxter Inn** (p58) and **Stitch** (p58). If you're not ready to call it a night, check out what's going down at **Good God Small Club** (p59).

 **Top Sights**

Art Gallery of NSW (p46)

**Local Life**

Meandering along Macquarie St (p48)

**Best of Sydney**

**Eating**

Sepia (p55)

Tetsuya's (p55)

Spice Temple (p56)

Rockpool Bar & Grill (p56)

Central Baking Depot (p56)

Chat Thai (p56)

**Markets**

Paddy's Markets (p63)

## Getting There

**Train** By far the best option for getting here, with stations at Central, Town Hall, Wynyard, Martin Place, St James and Museum.

**Bus** Numerous bus routes traverse the city centre. Railway Sq is a major stop.

**Light Rail** City stops include Central, Capitol Square and Paddy's Market; a handy option if you're coming from Glebe or Pyrmont.

## Top Sights
# Art Gallery of NSW

With its classical Greek frontage and modern rear end, the Art Gallery of NSW plays a prominent and gregarious role in Sydney society. Blockbuster international touring exhibitions arrive regularly (recent examples include Picasso and the Chinese terracotta warriors) and there's an outstanding permanent collection of Australian art, including a substantial indigenous collection. The gallery also plays host to a lively line-up of lectures, concerts, screenings, celebrity talks and children's activities.

👁 Map p50, E3

☎ 1800 679 278

www.artgallery.nsw.gov.au

Art Gallery Rd

admission free

🕐 10am-5pm Thu-Tue, to 9pm Wed

🚆 St James

Sol Le Witt's *Wall Drawing #1091: Arcs, Circles and Bands (room) 2003,* Art Gallery of NSW

# Don't Miss

### Australian Collection

As you enter, the galleries to the left are devoted to 20th- and 21st-century Australian works (featuring the likes of Sidney Nolan, Grace Cossington Smith and James Gleeson), while to the right the central room contains local 19th-century art (including Arthur Streeton's 1891 work, *Fire's on*). In the entrance court in the middle, look out for *The balcony 2* (1975), Brett Whiteley's luminous depiction of Sydney Harbour.

An absolute highlight is the Yiribana Gallery on the lowest level, containing a wonderful Aboriginal and Torres Strait Islander collection (including works by Binyinyuwuy, Tom Djawa and Brenda L Croft).

### European Collection

Also on the ground floor, the European art collection is split into two sections: 15th to 19th century (Constable, Gainsborough, Rubens) and 19th and 20th century (Degas, Van Gogh, Monet, Rodin).

### Asian Collection

Ceramics and religious art from the gallery's well-regarded Asian collection is displayed at the rear of the ground level. The remainder of the collection (Chinese, Korean and Japanese art) is on the first of the lower levels, by the cafe.

### Lower Level 2

Lower level 2 has the constantly changing contemporary (Gilbert & George, Jeff Koons, Sol LeWitt) and photography galleries. In the modern gallery, look out for Pablo Picasso's *Nude in a rocking chair* (1956) and Antony Gormley's sculpture *Haft* (2007).

## ☑ Top Tips

▶ A range of free, guided tours is offered on different themes and in various languages: enquire at the desk or check the website.

▶ The gallery's most famous annual show features entries in the unfailingly controversial Archibald Prize for portraiture, Wynne Prize for landscape painting or figure sculpture and Sulman Prize for subject or mural painting (usually in April and May; admission $10).

▶ Junior art-lovers can take a free self-guided iPod tour, follow tailored trails, and attend free performances (2.30pm Sundays).

## ✕ Take a Break

The gallery's excellent **restaurant** (☎ 9225 1819; www.trippaswhitegroup.com .au; 2-/3-courses $55/70; ☺lunch & high tea daily) is located at the rear of the entrance level.

There's a more informal cafe on the floor below.

## Local Life
# Meandering along Macquarie St

Sydney's two most imposing streets are Macquarie St, the centre of government, and intersecting with it, Martin Place, its financial heart. During the day they thrum to the beat of commerce and politics. This precinct is the legacy of two visionaries: convict and architect Francis Greenway, and the man who broke society strictures by commissioning him, Governor Lachlan Macquarie.

**❶ Inspect Hyde Park Barracks**
Greenway designed this squarish, decorously Georgian structure as convict quarters. It later became an immigration depot, women's asylum and law court. These days it's a fascinating (if not entirely cheerful) **museum** (☎8239 2311; www.hht.net.au; Queens Sq, Macquarie St; adult/child $10/5; ⏰9.30am-5pm; ℝSt James), focusing on the barracks' history. In 2010 it was one of the Australian convict sites

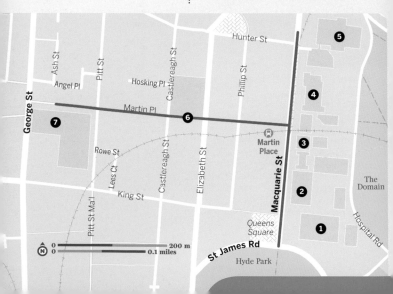

to be inscribed on the Unesco World Heritage List.

## ❷ Treasure the Mint

The stately **Mint** (☎8239 2288; www.hht .net.au; 10 Macquarie St; admission free; ⏲9am-5pm Mon-Fri; ⓂMartin Place) building (1816) was originally the southern wing of the infamous Rum Hospital, built by two Sydney merchants in return for a monopoly on the rum trade (Sydney's currency in those days). It became a branch of the Royal Mint in 1854, the first outside England.

## ❸ Admire Sydney Hospital

Australia's oldest **hospital** (☎9382 7111; www.seslhd.health.nsw.gov.au; 8 Macquarie St; ⓂMartin Place) has a grand Victorian sandstone facade and a peaceful central courtyard with a cafe and a kitsch enamelled swan fountain. In provocative recline out the front of the hospital is the pig-ugly bronze statue *Il Porcellino*. Rub its snout for luck.

## ❹ Visit Parliament

Built in 1816 as part of the Rum Hospital (along with its twin, the Mint), **Parliament House** (☎9230 2111; www .parliament.nsw.gov.au; 6 Macquarie St; admission free; ⏲9am-5pm Mon-Fri; ⓂMartin Place) has been home to the Parliament of New South Wales (NSW) since 1829, making it the world's oldest continually operating parliament building. You need to pass through a metal detector to access the assembly chambers, art exhibitions and historical displays.

## ❺ Study the State Library

The **State Library of NSW** (☎9273 1414; www.sl.nsw.gov.au; Macquarie St; admission free; ⏲9am-8pm Mon-Thu, to 5pm Fri, 10am-5pm Sat & Sun; ⓂMartin Place) holds more than five million tomes, including James Cook's and Joseph Banks' journals and Captain (later Governor) Bligh's log from the mutinous HMAV *Bounty*. The elegant main reading room is clad in milky marble.

## ❻ March down Martin Place

Studded with imposing edifices, long, lean Martin Place was closed to traffic in 1971, forming a terraced pedestrian mall. Once the corporate crowds go home, skateboarders and film crews converge upon the ramps, stairs and fountains. Near the George St end is the Cenotaph, commemorating Australia's war dead.

## ❼ Rehydrate in GPO Sydney

As iconic as the Opera House in its time (1874), this colonnaded Victorian palazzo has been gutted, stabbed with office towers and transformed into a Westin hotel, swanky shops, restaurants and bars. Under a staircase in the basement there is a small historical display and a pipe housing the dribbling remnants of the Tank Stream.

**For reviews see**

◎ Top Sights    p46
◉ Sights        p52
❌ Eating        p55
🍷 Drinking      p58
🎭 Entertainment p60
🛍 Shopping      p62

400 m
0.25 miles

Art Gallery
of NSW

9

The Domain

Royal Botanic Gardens

Shakespeare Pl

Museum of Sydney 5

Phillip La

Macquarie St

Hospital Rd

Prince Albert St

St Marys Rd

St Mary's Cathedral

Cook + Phillip Park

College St

3

Cathedral St

Riley St

Sir John Young Cres

Bridge St

Macquarie Place

Young St

Bent St

Phillip St

Bligh St

O'Connell St

Spring St

Hunter St

Bond St

14

15

Martin Place

St James' Church

Queens Square

6

St James

Elizabeth St

St James Rd

Archibald Memorial Fountain

Hyde Park

Elizabeth St

Grosvenor St

Dalley St

Lang Park

Abercrombie La

Jamison St

12

25

Margaret St

Curtin Pl

Ash St

Angel Pl

27 20 30

Hosking Pl

Martin Pl

37

Sydney Tower

40

38 Eye

4

Pitt St Mall

41

Great Synagogue

8

23

Wynyard

Wynyard Park

Carrington St

Wynyard La

21

York La

29

York St

George St

31

28

36

43

Market Row

Market St

24

Druitt St

Druitt Pl

11

Clarence St

22

Kent St

King St

19

Sussex St

Day St

16

Erskine St

Western Distributor

Hickson Rd

Shelley St

King Street Wharf

Lime St

Pyrmont Bridge

Wheat Rd

Cockle Bay Wharf

Cockle Bay

Bourke St

Flinders St

Bourke St

Campbell St

Little Bourke St

Crown St

Denham St

Crown St

Palmer St

Crown St

SURRY HILLS

Riley St

Stanley St

Sutton St

Eastbound Cross City Tunnel

Westbound Cross City Tunnel

Yurong St

Riley St

Burton St

Liverpool St

Francis St

Hargrave La

Charlotte La

Oxford St

Waine St

Ann St

Little Albion St

Hills Reserve

College St

Poplar St

Brisbane St

Harmony Park

Smith St

Batman La

Hunt St

Albion St

Park St

Hyde Park

Pool of Remembrance

Anzac Memorial

Museum

Wentworth Ave

Reservoir St

Mary St

Mary St

Nithsdale St

Foy La

Foster St

Elizabeth St

Castlereagh St

Bathurst St

Goulburn St

Campbell St

Hay St

Belmore Park

Central

Eddy Ave

Central

Central

Pitt St

Liverpool St

42

Wilmot St

Central St

City Host Information Kiosk

Town Hall

Town Hall

7

10

St Andrew's Cathedral

George St

Kent St

Albion Pl

35

32

Parker St

17

33

Rawson Pl

Railway Square

Druitt La

13

26

Eager St

18

Chinatown

Capitol Square

Thomas St

Sussex St

Dixon St

City Host Information Kiosk

2

39

HAYMARKET

Ultimo Rd

Day St

Harbour St

Western Distributor

Chinese Garden of Friendship

Tumbalong Park

Pier St

34

Paddy's Markets

Quay St

Darling Dr

Harris St

# Sights

### Hyde Park PARK

1 ⊙ Map p50, D5

Formal Hyde Park has manicured gardens and a tree-formed tunnel running down its spine, which looks particularly pretty at night, illuminated by fairy lights. The park's northern end is crowned by the **Archibald Memorial Fountain**, featuring Greek mythological figures, while at the other end, the shallow Pool of Remembrance fronts the art deco **Anzac Memorial** (☏9267 7668; www.rslnsw.com .au; Hyde Park; admission free; ⊙9am-5pm; ⍰Museum), commemorating the soldiers of the Australia and New Zealand Army Corps (Anzacs) who served in WWI. (Elizabeth St; ⍰St James & Museum)

### Chinatown NEIGHBOURHOOD

2 ⊙ Map p50, B7

Wedged into the Haymarket district, Chinatown is a tight nest of restaurants, shops and aroma-filled alleyways. No longer just Chinese, the area is truly pan-Asian. On Chinese New Year half of Sydney tries to squish into these tiny lanes. Dixon St is the heart and soul of Chinatown: a narrow pedestrian mall with ornate dragon gates *(paifang)* at either end. (www.chinatown .com.au/eng; Dixon St; ⍰Town Hall)

### St Mary's Cathedral CHURCH

3 ⊙ Map p50, D4

Built to last, this 106m-long Gothic Revival megalith was begun in 1868, consecrated in 1905 and substantially finished in 1928, but the 75m-high spires weren't added until 2000. The

---

## Understand
### Chinese in Australia

Chinese immigrants started to come to Australia around 1840 when convict transportation ceased and labouring jobs became freely available. Initially they were considered a solution to labour shortages, but as gold rush fever took hold, racial intolerance grew. The tireless Chinese were seen as threats, and state entry restrictions were enforced from the early 19th century into much of the 20th century.

In 1861 the NSW government enacted the 'White Australia Policy', aimed at reducing the influx of Chinese. This included a ban on naturalisation, work-permit restrictions and acts such as the 1861 Chinese Immigration Regulation & Restriction Act (an immigrant tax). The White Australia Policy wasn't completely dismantled until 1973.

Today people of Chinese heritage make up 7.9% of Sydney's population, with well over half of these born in Australia.

ANTHONY NG0 / GETTY IMAGES ©

Archibald Memorial Fountain in Hyde Park

crypt has an impressive terrazzo mosaic floor inspired by the Celtic-style illuminations of the *Book of Kells*. In the early morning and late afternoon the sun streams through the stained-glass windows. (9220 0400; www.st maryscathedral.org.au; cnr College St & St Marys Rd; ⊙6.30am-6.30pm; ☒St James)

### Sydney Tower Eye    TOWER

**4** ◎ Map p50, C3

The 309m-tall Sydney Tower (1981) offers 360-degree views from the observation level 250m up and even better ones for daredevils braving the Skywalk on its roof. The visit starts with the 4D Experience – a short 3D film giving you a bird's-eye view of city, surf, harbour and what lies beneath the water, accompanied by mist sprays and bubbles. (9333 9222; www .sydneytowereye.com.au; 100 Market St; adult/ child $25/20, Skywalk adult/child $65/45; ⊙9am-10.30pm; ☒St James)

### Museum of Sydney    MUSEUM

**5** ◎ Map p50, D1

Built on the site of Sydney's first (and infamously pungent) Government House, the MoS is a fragmented, story-telling museum using state-of-the-art installations to explore the city's people, places, cultures and evolution. The history of the indigenous Eora people is highlighted – touching on the millennia of continuous occupation of this place. Be sure to open some of the many stainless steel and glass drawers.

(MoS; ☑9251 5988; www.hht.net.au; cnr Phillip & Bridge Sts; adult/child $10/5; ⏱9.30am-5pm; 🚇Circular Quay)

## St James' Church CHURCH

6  Map p50, D3

Built from convict-made bricks, Sydney's oldest church (1819) is another Francis Greenway extravaganza. It was originally designed as a courthouse, but the brief changed: 'Hey Frank, we need an Anglican church!' The cells became the crypt. Check out the dark-wood choir loft, the sparkling copper dome, the crypt shop and the cool stained-glass 'Creation Window' from renovations in the 1950s. Free classical concerts are held at 1.15pm on Wednesdays between March and December. See the website or call for details on daily services. (☑8227 1300; www.sjks.org.au; 173 King St; ⏱10am-4pm Mon-Fri, 9am-1pm Sat, 7.30am-4pm Sun; 🚇St James)

## Town Hall NOTABLE BUILDING

7  Map p50, B5

Mansard roofs, sandstone turrets, wrought-iron trimmings and over-the-top balustrades: the High Victorian wedding-cake exterior of the Town Hall (built 1869–89) is something to behold. Inside, the elaborate chamber room and the wood-lined concert hall are almost as good; the concert hall has a humongous 8000-pipe organ and hosts free lunchtime concerts monthly. (☑9265 9189; www.cityofsydney.nsw.gov.au/sydneytownhall; 483 George St; ⏱8am-6pm Mon-Fri; 🚇Town Hall)

## Great Synagogue SYNAGOGUE

8  Map p50, C4

The heritage-listed Great Synagogue (1878) is the spiritual home of Sydney's oldest Jewish congregation, established in 1831. It's considered the Mother Synagogue of Australia and architecturally is the most important in the southern hemisphere, combining Romanesque, Gothic, Moorish and Byzantine elements. Tours include the AM Rosenblum Museum's artefacts and a video presentation on Jewish beliefs, traditions and history in Australia. (☑9267 2477; www.greatsynagogue.org.au; 187a Elizabeth St; tours adult/child $10/5; ⏱tours noon Tue & Thu; 🚇St James)

## The Domain PARK

9  Map p50, E3

Administered by the Royal Botanic Gardens, The Domain is a grassy tract east of Macquarie St where large-scale public events are held. Sculptures dot the park, including a reclining Henry Moore figure and Brett Whiteley's *Almost Once* (1991) – two giant matches, one burnt – rising near the Art Gallery. (www.rbgsyd.nsw.gov.au; Art Gallery Rd; 🚇St James)

## St Andrew's Cathedral CHURCH

10  Map p50, B5

Sporting beautiful stained glass and twin spires inspired by England's York Minster, squat St Andrew's Anglican is the oldest cathedral in Australia (1868). Music is a big deal here: free organ recitals are held on Fridays at 1.10pm and a concert band performs on alternate Wednesdays at 12.30pm. During school terms 'Young Music' concerts are held at 12.30pm on Mondays. (☎9265 1661; www.cathedral.sydney.anglican.asn.au; cnr George & Bathurst Sts; ⊙10am-4pm Mon, Tue, Fri & Sat, 8am-8pm Wed, 10am-6.30pm Thu, 7.30am-8pm Sun; ⊠Town Hall)

# Eating

## Sepia
JAPANESE, FUSION **$$$**

11  Map p50, A4

There's nothing washed out or brown-tinged about Sepia's food: Martin Benn's picture-perfect creations are presented in glorious Technicolor, with each taste worth a thousand words. A Japanese sensibility permeates the boundary-pushing menu, earning this relative newcomer the city's top dining gong in 2012. (☎9283 1990; www.sepiarestaurant.com.au; 201 Sussex St; mains $48, 4-courses $120; ⊙lunch Fri & Sat, dinner Tue-Sat; ⊠Town Hall)

## Est.
MODERN AUSTRALIAN **$$$**

12  Map p50, B1

Pressed-tin ceilings, huge columns, oversized windows and modern furniture make Est. a must-see for the interior design as much as the food. Seafood fills around half of the slots on Chef Peter Doyle's menu. At dinner, choose between a four-course 'chef's menu' and a seven-course 'tasting menu'. Sydney dining at its best; thick wallets and fancy threads a must.

(☎9240 3000; www.merivale.com; L1, 252 George St; lunch mains $55-57, 4-course dinner $150, degustation $175; ⊙lunch Mon-Fri, dinner Mon-Sat; ⊠Wynyard)

## Tetsuya's
FRENCH, JAPANESE **$$$**

13  Map p50, B5

Down a clandestine security driveway, Tetsuya's – rated as one of the top restaurants in the world – is for those seeking a culinary journey rather than a simple stuffed belly. Settle in for 12-plus courses of French- and Japanese-inflected food from the creative genius of Japanese-born Tetsuya Wakuda. Book way ahead. (☎9267 2900; www.tetsuyas.com; 529 Kent St; degustation $210; ⊙lunch Sat, dinner Tue-Sat; ⊠Town Hall)

### Local Life
### Yum Cha

Despite the larger restaurants seating literally hundreds of dumpling devotees, there always seems to be queues in Chinatown on weekend mornings for yum cha. Literally meaning 'drink tea', it's really an opportunity to gorge on small plates of dim sum, wheeled between the tables on trolleys. Popular places include **East Ocean** (Map p50, B6; ☎9212 4198; www.eastocean.com.au; 421 Sussex St; dishes $9-29; ⊙10am-2am; ⊠Central) and **Marigold Restaurant** (Map p50, B7; ☎9281 3388; www.marigold.com.au; L5, 683 George St; yum cha $15-25, banquet $30-48; ⊙10am-3pm & 5.30pm-midnight; ⊠Central).

## Top Tip

**Midnight Feasting**

If jetlag or other lifestyle choices leave you with the midnight munchies, Chinatown is the best place in the city to be. Restaurants, even some of the very best ones, open late here – we're talking 2am for Chat Thai and East Ocean, and on Dixon St, you can find noodles to slurp at any time of night. Just don't expect service with a smile at 5am.

### Spice Temple
CHINESE $$

**14** Map p50, C2

Tucked away in the basement of his Rockpool Bar & Grill, owner-chef Neil Perry runs this darkly atmospheric temple to the cuisine of China's western provinces, especially Sichuan, Yunnan, Hunan, Jiangxi, Guangxi and Xingjiang. Expect plenty of heat and lots of thrills. (☑8078 1088; www.rockpool.com; 10 Bligh St; dishes $15-45; ⏱lunch Mon-Fri, dinner Mon-Sat; ℝMartin Place)

### Rockpool Bar & Grill
STEAKHOUSE $$$

**15** Map p50, C2

You'll feel like a 1930s Manhattan stockbroker when you dine at this sleek operation in the art deco City Mutual Building. The bar is famous for its dry-aged, full-blood wagyu burger (make sure you order a side of the hand-cut fat chips), but carnivores will be equally enamoured with the succulent steaks served in the grill. (☑8078 1900; www.rockpool.com; 66 Hunter St; mains $25-115; ⏱lunch Mon-Fri, dinner Mon-Sat; ℝMartin Place)

### Central Baking Depot
BAKERY $

**16** Map p50, A2

Once upon a time the best bakeries were confined to the suburbs, but CBD has brought quality baked goods into the heart of the CBD. Drop by for a savoury snack (pies, sausage rolls, croissants, pizza slices, sandwiches), or a sweet treat with coffee. Seating is limited to a modest scattering of tables and a window bench. (CBD; www.centralbakingdepot.com.au; 37-39 Erskine St; baked goods $7-9; ⏱breakfast & lunch Mon-Sat; ℝWynyard)

### Chat Thai
THAI $

**17** Map p50, B7

Cooler than your average Thai joint, this Thaitown lynchpin is so popular that a list is posted outside for you to affix your name to should you want a table. Expat Thais flock here for the dishes that don't make it onto your average suburban Thai restaurant menu – particularly the more unusual sweets. (☑9211 1808; www.chatthai.com.au; 20 Campbell St; mains $10-19; ⏱10am-2am; ℝCentral)

### Mamak
MALAYSIAN $

**18** Map p50, B6

Get here early (from 5.30pm) if you want to get a table without queuing, because this eat-and-run Malaysian

OLIVER STREWE / GETTY IMAGES ©

Chinatown meal

joint is one of the most popular chea-pies in the city. The satays are cooked over charcoal and are particularly delicious when accompanied by a flaky golden roti. No bookings and BYO alcohol. (www.mamak.com.au; 15 Goulburn St; mains $6-17; ⊘lunch & dinner; 🚇Town Hall)

### Bistrode CBD

BRITISH $$$

19 🍴 Map p50, B3

Bistrode is a celebration of all things carnivorous, with a menu to chal-lenge the lily-livered. And the lily sure ain't gilded – it's more likely dipped in blood and used to garnish the 'lamb's heart and minds' that's on the menu. The food is exceptional: hearty and intricate with plenty of

kooky twists. (📞9240 3000; www .merivale.com; L1, 52 King St; mains $37-40; ⊘lunch & dinner Mon-Fri; 🚇Wynyard)

### Felix

FRENCH $$

20 🍴 Map p50, C2

Waiters bustle about in black ties and long aprons in this *très traditionnel* French bistro, with Parisian subway tiles on the walls and a solid list of tried and true classics on the menu. If you feel the urge to work off your *coq au vin* in *le discothèque* later, the Ivy is upstairs. (📞9240 3000; www .merivale.com; 2 Ash St; mains $28-32; ⊘lunch Mon-Fri, dinner Mon-Sat; 🚇Wynyard)

# Drinking

## Stitch

BAR

**21** Map p50, B2

The finest exemplar of Sydney's vogue for fake speakeasies, Stitch is accessed via swinging doors at the rear of what looks like a tailor's workshop. Hidden beneath is a surprisingly large but perpetually crowded space, decorated with sewing patterns and wooden Singer cases. A charming maître d' manages the inevitable wait for a booth seat with considerable skill; the food's excellent, too. (www.stitchbar.com; 61 York St; 4pm-midnight Mon & Tue, 4pm-2am Wed & Sat, noon-2am Thu & Fri; Wynyard)

## Baxter Inn

BAR

**22** Map p50, B3

Yes, it really is down that dark lane and through that unmarked door (it's easier to find if there's a queue; otherwise look for the bouncer lurking nearby). Whisky's the poison at this particular speakeasy. Despite the bowties and comedy hipster moustaches, the friendly barmen really know their stuff and can help you select from the huge list. (www.thebaxterinn.com; 156 Clarence St; 4pm-1am Mon-Sat; Town Hall)

## Bambini Wine Room

WINE BAR

**23** Map p50, C4

Don't worry, this bar doesn't sell wine to *bambinis* – it's a very

---

### Understand
### The Rum Rebellion

When Governor Phillip returned to England in 1792, Francis Grose took over. Grose granted land to officers of the New South Wales Corps, nicknamed the Rum Corps. With so much money, land and cheap labour in their hands, this military leadership made huge profits at the expense of small farmers. They began paying for labour and local products in rum. Meeting little resistance (everyone was drunk), they managed to upset, defy, outmanoeuvre and outlast three governors, the last of which was William Bligh, the famed captain of the mutinous ship HMAV *Bounty*. In 1808 the Rum Corps ousted Bligh from power in what became known as the Rum Rebellion.

The Rum Rebellion was the final straw for the British government – in 1809 it decided to punish its unruly child. Lieutenant Colonel Lachlan Macquarie was dispatched with his own regiment and ordered the New South Wales Corps to return to London to get their knuckles rapped. Having broken the stranglehold of the Rum Corps, Governor Macquarie began laying the groundwork for social reforms.

grown-up, European affair. The tiny dark-wood-panelled room is the sort of place where you'd expect to see Oscar Wilde holding court in the corner. There's an extensive wine list, slick table service, free almonds and breadsticks, and disembodied, postmodern cornices dangling from above. (☎9283 7098; www.bambinitrust .com.au; 185 Elizabeth St; ⏱3-10pm Mon-Fri, 5.30-11pm Sat; ☒St James)

## Grandma's
COCKTAIL BAR

24 ☻ Map p50, B4

Billing itself as a 'retrosexual haven of cosmopolitan kitsch and faded granny glamour', Grandma's hits the mark. A stag's head greets you on the stairs and ushers you into a tiny sub-terranean world of parrot wallpaper and tiki cocktails. Someone's supris-ingly cool granny must be very proud. (www.grandmasbarsydney.com; basement, 275 Clarence St; ⏱3pm-midnight Mon-Thu, noon-1am Fri, 5pm-1am Sat; ☒Town Hall)

## Orbit
COCKTAIL BAR

25 ☻ Map p50, C1

Shoot up to this murderously cool re-volving *Goldfinger*-esque bar, offering killer cocktails and views to die for. Sink into an Eero Saarinen tulip chair and sip a kung fu mojito while all of Sydney is paraded before you. (☎9247 9777, www.summitrestaurant.com.au; L47, Australia Square, 264 George St; ⏱10am-late Mon-Fri, 5pm-late Sat & Sun; ☒Wynyard)

## Good God Small Club
CLUB, LIVE MUSIC

26 ☻ Map p50, B6

In a defunct underground taverna near Chinatown, Good God's rear dancetaria hosts everything from live indie bands to Jamaican reggae, '50s soul, rockabilly and tropical house music. Its success lies in the focus on great music rather than glamorous surrounds. (www.goodgodgoodgod.com; 55 Liverpool St; front bar free, club free-$20; ⏱5pm-1am Wed, 5pm-2am Thu, 5pm-5am Fri, 6pm-5am Sat; ☒Town Hall)

## Establishment
BAR

Establishment's cashed-up crush proves that the art of swilling cocktails after a hard city day is not lost. Sit at the majestic marble bar, in the swish courtyard or be absorbed by a leather lounge as stockbrokers scribble their phone numbers on the backs of coasters for flirty city chicks. Located at Est. (see 12 ☻ Map p50, B1). (☎9240 3100; www.merivale.com; ground level, 252 George St; ⏱11am-late Mon-Fri, 6pm-late Sat; ☒Wynyard)

## Ivy
BAR, CLUB

27 ☻ Map p50, B2

Hidden down a laneway off George St, the Ivy is a supersexy complex featuring bars, restaurants, discreet lounges...even a swimming pool. It's also Sydney's most hyped venue; expect lengthy queues of suburban kids teetering on infeasibly high heels, waiting to shed $20 for the privilege of entry on a Saturday night. (☎9254 8100; www.merivale.com; L1, 330 George St; admission free-$20; ☺11am-late Mon-Fri, 5pm-late Sat; ☒Wynyard)

### Marble Bar                    BAR, LIVE MUSIC

28  Map p50, B4

Built for a staggering £32,000 in 1893 as part of the Adams Hotel on Pitt St, this ornate underground bar is one of the best places in town for putting on the ritz (even if this is the Hilton). When the Adams was demolished in 1968, every marble slab, wood carving and bronze capital was dismantled, restored, then reassembled here. (☎9265 2000; www.marblebarsydney.com .au; basement, Hilton Hotel, 488 George St; ☺4pm-midnight Sun-Thu, 3pm-2am Fri & Sat; ☒Town Hall)

### Grasshopper                    BAR

29  Map p50, B3

The first of many grungy laneway bars to open in the inner city, Grasshopper couldn't have chosen a more darkly ironic location than Temperance Lane. The heart of the operation is the cool downstairs bar; hop upstairs for food. (www.thegrasshopper.com.au; 1 Temperance Lane; ☺noon-late Mon-Fri, 5.30pm-late Sat; ☒St James)

# Entertainment

### City Recital Hall          PERFORMANCE VENUE

30  Map p50, C2

Based on the classical configuration of the 19th-century European concert hall, this custom-built 1200-seat venue boasts near-perfect acoustics. Catch top-flight companies such as **Musica Viva** (☎8394 6666; www.mva.org.au; tickets $30-86), the **Australian Brandenburg Orchestra** (☎9328 7581; www.brandenburg .com.au; tickets $28-167) and the **Australian Chamber Orchestra** (☎8274 3888; www.aco.com.au; tickets $37-129) performing here. (☎8256 2222; www.cityrecitalhall .com; 2 Angel Pl; tickets $20-92; ☺box office 9am-5pm Mon-Fri; ☒Martin Place)

### State Theatre          PERFORMANCE VENUE

31  Map p50, B4

The beautiful 2000-seat State Theatre is a lavish, gilt-ridden, chandelier-dangling palace. It hosts the **Sydney Film Festival** (☎9318 0999; www.sff.org .au) in early June, concerts, comedy, opera, musicals and the odd celebrity chef. (☎136 100; www.statetheatre.com.au; 49 Market St; tickets $60-235; ☺box office 9am-5pm Mon-Fri; ☒St James)

### Metro Theatre          PERFORMANCE VENUE

32  Map p50, B6

Easily Sydney's best venue to catch local and alternative international acts (The Maccabees, Public Enemy, Ladyhawke) in well-ventilated, easy-

State Theatre

viewing comfort. Other offerings include comedy, cabaret and dance parties. (☎9550 3666; www.metrotheatre.com.au; 624 George St; tickets $29-100; Town Hall)

## Capitol Theatre PERFORMANCE VENUE

33 ⭐ Map p50, B7

Lavishly restored, this large city theatre is home to long-running musicals (*The Lion King, A Chorus Line*) and the occasional big name concert (Diana Ross, Chris Isaak). (☎9320 5000; www.capitoltheatre.com.au; 13 Campbell St; tickets $59-199; ⏱box office 9am-5pm Mon-Fri; Ⓡ Central)

## Sydney Entertainment Centre PERFORMANCE VENUE

34 ⭐ Map p50, A7

A big 12,000-seat concrete box between Chinatown and Darling Harbour, purpose-built for superstar extravaganzas (Radiohead, The Black Keys, The Wiggles). (☎9320 4200, www.sydentcent.com.au; 35 Harbour St; tickets $89-130; Ⓡ Central)

## Event Cinemas George St CINEMA

35 ⭐ Map p50, B5

An orgy of popcorn-fuelled mainstream entertainment, this monster movie palace has 18 screens and

WIBOWO RUSLI / GETTY IMAGES ©

Queen Victoria Building

plenty of eateries and teen-centric distractions. All tickets are $11 on Tuesdays. (📞9273 7300; www.event cinemas.com.au; 505 George St; adult/child $19/14; ⏱9.30am-midnight; 🚊Town Hall)

# Shopping

## Queen Victoria Building

SHOPPING CENTRE

**36** 🔒 Map p50, B4

Unbelievably, this High Victorian masterpiece (1898) was repeatedly slated for demolition before it was restored in the mid-1980s. Occupying an entire city block, the QVB is a Venetian Romanesque temple to the gods of retail. Sure, the 200 specialty shops are great, but check out the

wrought-iron balconies, the stained-glass shopfronts, the mosaic floors and the replica crown jewels. (QVB; 📞9264 9209; www.qvb.com.au; 455 George St; ⏱11am-5pm Sun, 9am-6pm Mon-Wed, Fri & Sat, 9am-9pm Thu; 🚊Town Hall)

## Strand Arcade

SHOPPING CENTRE

**37** 🔒 Map p50, B3

Constructed in 1891, the Strand rivals the QVB in the ornateness stakes. Three floors of designer fashions, Australiana and old-world coffee shops will make your short cut through here considerably longer. Top Australian designers commune and collude on the upper levels. (www.strandarcade.com.au; 412 George St; ⏱9am-5.30pm Mon-Wed & Fri, 9am-8pm Thu, 9am-4pm Sat, 11am-4pm Sun; 🚊St James)

## Westfield Sydney

MALL

**38** 🔒 Map p50, C3

The city's newest shopping mall is a bafflingly large complex gobbling up Sydney Tower and a fair chunk of Pitt St Mall. They've upped the glamour by ensnaring some of the city's top restaurants into spaces adjacent to the excellent food court. (www.westfield.com.au/sydney; cnr Pitt St Mall & Market St)

## Paddy's Markets

MARKET

**39** 🔒 Map p50, A7

Cavernous, 1000-stall Paddy's is the Sydney equivalent of Istanbul's Grand Bazaar, but swap the hookahs and carpets for mobile-phone covers, Eminem T-shirts and cheap sneakers. Pick up a

Top Tip
## City Shopping

Sydneysiders head cityward when they've got something special to buy or some serious retail therapy is required. The city centre's up-market stores – centred on Pitt St Mall – offer plenty of choice. Shopping is one of Chinatown's big drawcards, with countless bargains of the 'Made in China/Taiwan/Korea' variety.

VB singlet for Uncle Bruce or wander the aisles in capitalist awe. (www.paddysmarkets.com.au; 9-13 Hay St; ⊙9am-5pm Wed-Sun; ⑤Central)

### David Jones                    DEPARTMENT STORE

**40**  Map p50, C3

In two enormous city buildings, DJs is Sydney's premier department store. The Castlereagh St store has womens· and childrenswear; Market St has menswear, electrical goods and a high-brow food court. (☑9266 5544; www.davidjones.com.au; 86-108 Castlereagh St; ⊙9.30am-7pm Sat-Wed, 9.30am-9pm Thu & Fri; ⑤St James)

### Myer                    DEPARTMENT STORE

**41**  Map p50, B3

At seven storeys, Myer (formerly Grace Bros) is one of Sydney's largest stores and a prime venue for after-Christmas sales. It's marginally less swanky than David Jones, but you'll still find plenty of high-quality goods and some slick cafes. (☑9238 9111; www.myer.com.au; 436 George St; ⊙9am-7pm Fri-Wed, 9am-9pm Thu; ⑤St James)

### Red Eye Records                    MUSIC

**42**  Map p50, C6

Sells a rampaging collection of classic, rare and collectable records, CDs, books, posters and music DVDs. New music is at the branch at 143 York St. (☑9262 9755; www.redeye.com.au; 370 Pitt St; ⊙9am-6pm Mon-Fri, to 9pm Thu, to 5pm Sat; ⑤Museum)

### Kinokuniya                    BOOKS

**43**  Map p50, B4

This outpost of the Japanese chain is the largest bookstore in Sydney, with more than 300,000 titles. The comics section is a magnet for geeky teens – the imported Chinese, Japanese and European magazine section isn't. There's a cool little cafe here, too. (☑9262 7996; www.kinokuniya.com; L2, The Galeries, 500 George St; ⊙10am-7pm Fri-Wed, 10am-9pm Thu; ⑤Town Hall)

Explore

# Darling Harbour & Pyrmont

Darling Harbour was once a thriving dockland, chock-full of factories, warehouses and shipyards. After decades of decline it was reinvented as a dedicated entertainment district, opening for the bicentennial in 1988. Dotted between the flyovers and fountains are some of the city's highest profile attractions, while every other inch of the waterline is given over to bars and restaurants.

# The Sights in a Day

☀️ Start early with the morning tour of the **Sydney Fish Market** (p72) and then catch the light rail to Exhibition stop. Take a peaceful stroll through the **Chinese Garden of Friendship** (p69) and then cross through **Tumbalong Park** (p71) to the western side of Darling Harbour. Spend the rest of the morning inspecting the ships, submarine and displays at the **Australian National Maritime Museum** (p69). For lunch, head to The Star's cafe court for dumplings at **Din Tai Fung** (p72), followed by a sweet treat at **Adriano Zumbo** (p72) or **Messina** (p72).

☀️ Across Pyrmont Bridge you'll find plenty to keep you (and the kids) amused for the rest of the afternoon. Three attractions are packed cheek-by-jowl; start with the **Sydney Aquarium** (p66) and then – if you have the time, budget and inclination – tackle **Wild Life Sydney** (p71) and **Madame Tussauds** (p71).

🌙 Have a sunset cocktail at **Flying Fish** (p74) then head on to **Zaafran** (p71) for fine Indian dining. Work off your meal with a stroll around the water's edge, watching the lights dancing on the water.

 **Top Sights**

Sydney Aquarium (p66)

💜 **Best of Sydney**

**Eating**

Adriano Zumbo (p72)

**Green Spaces**

Chinese Garden of Friendship (p69)

Tumbalong Park (p71)

**With Kids**

Sydney Aquarium (p66)

Madame Tussauds (p71)

## Getting There

🚆 **Train** Walk down to Darling Harbour from Wynyard or Town Hall stations.

🚋 **Light Rail** From Central or Glebe, the light rail is your best option. Stops include Exhibition, Convention, Pyrmont Bay, The Star and Fish Market.

⛴ **Ferry** Boats head from Circular Quay to Darling Harbour and Pyrmont Bay.

🚌 **Bus** Bus 443 heads from Circular Quay to the Maritime Museum.

## Top Sights
# Sydney Aquarium

Even with its hefty admission charges, this place brings in more paying visitors than any other attraction in Australia. Aside from regular wall-mounted tanks and ground-level enclosures, there are two large pools that you can walk through, safely enclosed in perspex tunnels, as an intimidating array of sharks and rays pass overhead. Residents of the penguin enclosure have lawless amounts of fun, while moon jellyfish billow through their disco-lit tube and an octopus keeps a wary eye on proceedings. Needless to say, kids love it.

Map p68, D3

82517800

www.sydneyaquarium
.com.au

1–5 Wheat Rd

adult/child $35/20

9am-8pm

Town Hall

Sydney Aquarium

# Don't Miss

### Sharks

Sharks get a bad rap, and one of the aquarium's biggest educational ambitions is to change perceptions of these misunderstood and endangered creatures. Mind you, coming up close to the impressive dentistry of the grey nurse sharks as they glide overhead will do little to allay fears.

### Dugongs

The aquarium's two dugongs were rescued when washed up on different Queensland beaches. After attempts to return the male to the wild failed, the decision was made to keep them in captivity; there are only a handful of these large marine mammals in captivity worldwide.

### Japanese Spider Crabs

Forget the sharks, these giants from the deep are much creepier. The aquarium's specimens are mere tiddlers – they can grow to 4m claw to claw.

### Great Barrier Reef

The colourful finale of the complex is this large tank (two million litres) filled with representatives of the multitude of creatures that inhabit Australia's most famous ecosystem. Sharks, sawfish, lobsters, clownfish, lionfish, angelfish, triggerfish, transsexual wrasses and swoonworthy DayGlo corals all come together in the final floor-to-ceiling 'reef theatre'. Sit down and watch the show..

### Talks & Feeds

Throughout the day there's a roster of scheduled talks in six different parts of the complex, with the highlights being the mid-afternoon penguin and shark feed (in separate enclosures, naturally!) and the late morning shark feed in the Great Barrier Reef tank.

☑ **Top Tips**

▶ Sydney Aquarium, Wild World Sydney, Madame Tussauds, Sydney Tower Eye and Manly Oceanworld are all run by the same company. You'll save a pretty penny on admission by purchasing combo tickets, which are available in almost every permutation of attractions.

▶ Arrive early to beat the crowds.

▶ Booking online will save you a few dollars.

▶ Disabled access is good.

✕ **Take a Break**

On the edge of the King Street Wharf complex nearest to the Aquarium, Cargo Bar (p75) offers light snacks.

A similar distance in the opposite direction, Pontoon (p75) also serves casual meals.

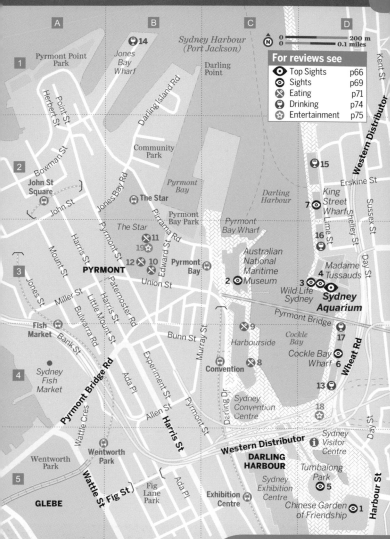

SANDRA LUCAS / CREAMSTIME.COM ©

Chinese Garden of Friendship

# Sights

### Chinese Garden of Friendship

GARDENS

1  Map p68, D5

Built according to Taoist principles, the Chinese Garden of Friendship is an oasis of tranquility. Designed by architects from Guangzhou (Sydney's sister city) for Australia's bicentenary in 1988, the garden interweaves pavilions, waterfalls, lakes, paths and lush plant life. It's too serene for words. (☏9240 8888; www.chinesegarden.com.au; Harbour St; adult/child/family $6/3/15, audioguide $4; ⏰9.30am-5.30pm; 🚇Town Hall)

### Australian National Maritime Museum

MUSEUM

2  Map p68, C3

Beneath an Utzon-like roof (a low-rent Opera House?), the Maritime Museum sails through Australia's inextricable relationship with the sea. Exhibitions range from Aboriginal canoes to surf culture, to the navy. There are free tours every day and kids' activities on Sundays. The 'big ticket' (adult/child $25/10) includes the vessels moored outside, including a submarine, destroyer and an 1874 square rigger. (☏9298 3777; www.anmm.gov.au; 2 Murray St; adult/child $7/3.50; ⏰9.30am-5pm; 🚇Pyrmont Bay)

## Understand
# Beyond a Working Harbour

### Building a Bustling Port
Sydney has always relied on its harbour. All sorts of cargo (including human, in the form of convicts) has been unloaded here, and some of the more interesting Sydney buildings are the utilitarian wharves and warehouses still lining parts of the harbour's inner shores. After the bubonic plague arrived in Sydney in 1900 (killing 103 Sydneysiders), the government took control of the old, privately owned wharves. Many ageing, neoclassical warehouses were razed and replaced with new structures, some of them surprisingly elegant.

### Decline & Reinvigoration
The 'containerisation' of shipping in the 1960s and '70s and the move of port activity to Botany Bay made many of the Edwardian wharves redundant almost overnight. Now, Sydneysiders' obsession for harbour-side living is also putting many of these historic sites at risk. Fortunately, some have been transformed through inspired redevelopment – once-dilapidated sheds morphing into top-notch cafes, restaurants and apart-ments. Woolloomooloo's Finger Wharf, and the Walsh Bay and Pyrmont wharves are classic examples.

### Challenges
One of Sydney's big architectural challenges is to retain the rich heritage of a working harbour and to ensure these industrial sites have a successful role in the modern city. Critics condemn today's Darling Har-bour as a tacky Las Vegan aberration, but few fail to be amazed at how completely this once-disused industrial space has been transformed. The state government has Darling Harbour in its sights once again, with a major redevelopment planned for the Exhibition and Convention Centres. Depending on when you visit, you might find it, once again, a work in progress.

### Wild Life Sydney

ZOO

3 ● Map p68, D3

Complementing its sister and neighbour Sydney Aquarium, this large complex houses an impressive collection of Australian native reptiles, butterflies, spiders, snakes and mammals. The nocturnal section is particularly good, bringing out the extrovert in the quolls, potaroos, echidnas and possums, but the kids may be more interested in holding snakes and posing with koalas. (☎9333 9288; www.wildlifesydney.com.au; 1-5 Wheat Rd; adult/child $35/20; ☺9am-6pm Apr-Nov, 9am-8pm Dec-Mar; ☐Town Hall)

### Madame Tussauds

MUSEUM

4 ● Map p68, D3

In this celebrity-obsessed age, it's hardly surprising that Madame Tussauds' hyper-realistic waxwork dummies are just as popular now as when the eponymous madame lugged her macabre haul of French revolution death masks to London in 1803. Where else do mere mortals get to cosy up to Kylie and Hugh Jackman? (www.madametussauds.com/sydney; Aquarium Pier; adult/child $35/20; ☺9am-8pm; ☐Town Hall)

### Tumbalong Park

PARK

5 ● Map p68, D5

Flanked by the new Darling Walk development, this grassy circle on Darling Harbour's southern rump is set up for family fun. Sunbakers and frisbee-throwers occupy the lawns, while tourists dunk their feet in fountains on hot summer afternoons. There's also an excellent children's playground with a rubber floor (in case the kids don't bounce) and a 21m flying fox. (☐Town Hall)

### Cockle Bay Wharf

NOTABLE BUILDING

6 ● Map p68, D4

The first vaguely tasteful development to open in Darling Harbour, Cockle Bay Wharf occupies the harbour's cityside frontage as far as Pyrmont Bridge. Its sharp, contemporary angles are softened by the use of timber and whimsical sculptures; we particularly like the jaunty dancing storks. (www.cocklebaywharf.com; ☐Town Hall)

### King Street Wharf

NOTABLE BUILDINGS

7 ● Map p68, D2

Cockle Bay Wharf in ultramodern metal drag, the $800-million King St Wharf continues the Darling Harbour precinct north beyond Pyrmont Bridge. (www.ksw.com.au; Lime St; ☐Wynyard)

## Eating

### Zaaffran

INDIAN $$

8  Map p68, C4

In a city with a gazillion cheap Indian joints, Zaaffran is a stand-out. Authentic and innovative curries by chef Vikrant Kapoor (of Singapore's Raffles fame) are served up with awesome views across Darling Harbour's sparkle and sheen. Book a balcony seat and launch yourself into the tiger prawn coconut curry. Good vegetarian selection, too. (☑9211 8900; www.zaaffran.com.au; L2, Harbourside; mains $19-30; ☺lunch & dinner; ☑; ☒Convention)

### Kazbah
NORTH AFRICAN $$

9 🍽 Map p68, C4

Kazbah is known for beautifully presented, tasty dishes from the Maghreb and Middle East. The breakfasts are legendary, whether you opt for the exotic (sweet couscous, breakfast tagine) or the tried and true (eggs benedict, pancakes), and the tagines are exceptional at any time of day. (☑9555 7067; www.kazbah.com.au; The Promenade, Harbourside; breakfast $15-22, lunch $21-26, dinner $31-38; ☺breakfast, lunch & dinner; ☒Convention)

### Adriano Zumbo
PATISSERIE $

10 🍽 Map p68, B3

Australia's leading pastry chef has indulged his Willy Wonka fantasies in this concept store, with everything artfully displayed amid pastel colours and pink neon. Take away or sit down at the dessert train. (www.adrianozumbo.com; ground floor, The Star, 80 Pyrmont St; sweets $2.50 10; ☺11am-9pm Sun, 11am-11pm Mon-Sat; ☒The Star)

---

## ◯ Local Life
## Sydney Fish Market

The **Sydney Fish Market** (Map p68, A4; ☑9004 1100; www.sydneyfishmarket.com.au; Bank St; ☺7am-4pm; ☒Fish Market) shifts more than 15 million kilograms of seafood annually, and has restaurants, a deli, wine centre and an oyster bar. Chefs, locals and overfed seagulls vie for the day's catch. Check out the early-morning auctions on a behind-the-scenes **tour** (☑9004 1143; adult/child $20/10; ☺6.40am Mon, Thu & Fri), or sign up for a cooking class.

---

### Din Tai Fung
CHINESE $

11 🍽 Map p68, B3

While it also does noodles and buns, it's the dumplings which made this Taiwanese chain famous, delivering an explosion of fabulously flavoursome broth as you bite into the delicate casings. (ground floor, The Star, 80 Pyrmont St; mains $10-15; ☒The Star)

### Messina
ICE CREAM $

12 🍽 Map p68, B3

Join the queues waiting to sample Sydney's best gelato, in quirky flavours such as figs in Marsala and salted caramel. (www.gelatomessina.com; ground floor, The Star, 80 Pyrmont St; 2 scoops $5; ☒The Star)

## Understand
# Food Culture

- - - - - - - - - - - - - - - - - - - - - - - - - - - - - - - - -

### Modern Australian

Those making the case for a distinctly Australian cuisine might point to 'bush tucker' or a degustation menu of pavlova, lamingtons, Vegemite sandwiches and Anzac biscuits. Patriots might suggest eating the coat of arms: kangaroo and emu, with a crocodile starter. A more reasoned approach has been taken by Australia's more innovative chefs, reverting to convict stereotypes: eyeing the surroundings, determining what to steal and weaving it all into something better than the sum of its parts – something perfect for the location and the climate.

This mix of European traditions with exotic flavours is casually termed Modern Australian cuisine – an amalgamation of Mediterranean, Asian, Middle Eastern and Californian cooking practices that emphasise lightness, experimentation and healthy eating. It's a hybrid style, shaped by migrant influences, climatic conditions and local ingredients – a culinary adventure built around local, seasonal produce that plays freely with imported ingredients and their accompanying cooking techniques and traditions. In Sydney this light-fingered culinary style has filtered down from sophisticated restaurants to modest main street bistros and pubs.

The once ubiquitous phrase 'Mod Oz' may have fallen out of vogue, but the style of cooking is very much alive and well.

### Current Trends

A craze for Latin American street food has seen tangy soft-shell tacos replace salt and pepper squid as the bar snack of choice in hipper establishments. A similar fad for 'dude food' has seen posh places adding fancy burgers (called 'sliders' by those chefs who watch far too much American TV), pulled-pork sandwiches and big slabs of meat to their menus, often with a liberal side-serve of irony.

In an extension of the tapas trend that's been rolling for several years, 'shared plates' are all the rage. Bigger than tapas and not necessarily Spanish, this style of eating favours groups with adventurous palates. Fussy eaters and those from cultures which prefer their own portions on their own plates (we're looking at you, Brits) might find it more challenging.

Lyric Theatre, The Star

# Drinking

## Home

CLUB, LIVE MUSIC

13 Map p68, D4

Welcome to the pleasuredome: a three-level, 2100-capacity timber and glass 'prow' that's home to a dance floor, countless bars, outdoor balconies, and sonics that make other clubs sound like transistor radios. Catch top-name international DJs, plus live bands amping it up at Tokio Hotel downstairs from Tuesday to Saturday. (☎9266 0600; www.homesydney.com; 1 Wheat Rd, Cockle Bay Wharf; admission free-$55; ☾club Fri & Sat; ☒Town Hall)

## Flying Fish

COCKTAIL BAR

14 Map p68, B1

Beyond the architects and investment groups along Jones Bay Wharf is this romantic restaurant bar. The city lights work their magic all too easily here, aided by an indulgent cocktail list (from $18). Aside from all that romance stuff, it has the coolest toilets in town - the clear-glass stalls frost over when you close the door. (☎9518 6677; www.flyingfish.com.au; Jones Bay Wharf; ☾noon-5pm Sun, 6-10.30pm Mon-Sat; ☒The Star)

## Loft

BAR

**15**  Map p68, D2

The Loft is far from lofty – it's more like an open-plan office space – but the walls fold back and disappear, drawing your eyes out across Darling Harbour and beyond. Interior design is Moroccan chic and service is snappy. Book for high tea at high noon on Saturday and Sunday. Live music on Fridays. (☏9299 4770; www.theloftsydney .com; 3 Lime St, King St Wharf; ☺4pm-1am Mon-Thu, noon-3am Fri & Sat, noon-1am Sun; ⓡWynyard)

## Cargo Bar

BAR

**16**  Map p68, D3

This pioneering Darling Harbour bar still lures beautiful boys, babes and backpackers, who get wall-to-wall boozy after 11pm. DJs and live bands fire things up. Before the drinkers descend, savour the harbour views, tasty pizzas and salads. (☏9262 1777; www .cargobar.com.au; 52 The Promenade, King St Wharf; ☺11am-late; ⓡWynyard)

## Pontoon

BAR, DJ

**17**  Map p68, D4

Perennially busy Pontoon offers water breezes, cool tunes and high-tech sound and screens. The crowd is less appealing – with rugby necks, back-slapping office bully boys and deep-cleavaged 50-somethings – but it's still a reliable place for a beer and DJs from Thursday to Sunday. (☏9267 7099; www.pontoonbar.com; The Promenade North, Cockle Bay Wharf; ☺11am-midnight Sun-Wed, to 3am Thu-Sat; ⓡTown Hall)

# Entertainment

## IMAX Cinema

CINEMA

**18**  Map p68, D4

It's big bucks for a 45-minute movie, but everything about IMAX is big, and this is reputedly the largest IMAX in the world. The eight-storey screen shimmers with kid-friendly documentaries (sharks, Mars, haunted castles etc) as well as blockbuster features, many in 3D. Size matters. (☏9281 3300; www.imax .com.au; 31 Wheat Rd; adult/child from \$21/16; ☺sessions 10am-8.15pm; ⓡTown Hall)

## The Star

CASINO

**19**  Map p68, B3

After a name change and a \$961 million renovation, The Star reopened in late 2011 amid much hype. The complex includes high-profile restaurants, bars, a nightclub, an excellent food court, a light-rail station and the kind of high-end stores that will quickly gobble any winnings you might make. The 2000-seat Lyric Theatre stages musicals and the occasional concert. (www.star.com.au; 80 Pyrmont Rd; ☺24hr; ⓡThe Star)

Explore

# Inner West

The Inner West is a sociological stew of students, goths, urban hippies, artists, Aborigines, Mediterranean immigrants and sexual subculturalists. Newtown shadows King St, lined with funky boutiques, bookshops, yoga studios, cafes and an inordinate number of Thai restaurants. It's definitely climbing the social rungs, but Newtown is still free-thinking and bolshy. Glebe is similar, if a little quieter.

# The Sights in a Day

 Begin your day at the **Power-house Museum** (p82), where there's more than enough to keep you occupied for most of the morning. Catch the light rail to the Jubilee stop and pay a quick visit to **Sze Yup Temple** (p83) before walking around **Jubilee & Bicentennial Parks** (p83) to Blackwattle Bay. If you feel like indulging, stop at the **Boathouse on Blackwattle Bay** (p84) for lunch.

 Catch a cab to the **White Rabbit** (p82) gallery, then hop up to Newtown where you can spend the remainder of the afternoon shopping on King St. Take a short detour down Church St to explore the cobwebby corners of **Camperdown Cemetery** (p82).

 Grab dinner on King St. If you're not booked for a show at **Carriageworks** (p82), hit the local bars. A short pub-crawl route could include **Jester Seeds** (p87), **Corridor** (p88), the **Bank** (p86), **Zanzibar** (p88) and the **Courthouse** (p87). Or continue on to the **Sando** (p87) to catch a band, or to the **Imperial** (p88) for the Priscilla drag show.

For a local's day in the Inner West, see p78.

## ○ Local Life

Studying the University of Sydney (p78)

## ♥ Best of Sydney

**Bars & Pubs**
Bank Hotel (p86)

Courthouse Hotel (p87)

**With Kids**
Powerhouse Museum (p82)

**Gay & Lesbian**
Imperial Hotel (p88)

Bank Hotel (p86)

**For Free**
White Rabbit (p82)

Nicholson Museum (p79)

## Getting There

🚆 **Train** Newtown is particularly well served by trains, with four stations (Macdonaldtown, Newtown, Erskineville and St Peters) on three train lines (Inner West, South and Bankstown).

🚊 **Light Rail** Glebe has two MLR stops in its back streets (Glebe and Jubilee Park).

🚌 **Bus** Dozens of buses from the city ply Glebe Point Rd, Parramatta Rd and City Rd/King St.

# Local Life
# Studying the University of Sydney

Australia's oldest tertiary institution (1850) has more than 45,000 students and even boasts its own postcode. You don't need to have a PhD to grab a free campus map and wander around. The University completely dominates the surrounding suburbs of Camperdown, Darlington, Chippendale, and to a lesser extent, Glebe and Newtown.

**1 Scope out the Seymour Centre**

Behind a glass curtain wall on an insanely busy intersection, the Sydney Uni–affiliated **Seymour Centre** (☏9351 7940; www.seymourcentre.com.au; cnr City Rd & Cleveland St; tickets $16-65; ⊗box office 9am-6pm Mon-Fri, 11am-3pm Sat; ℝRedfern) shows an eclectic selection of plays, cabaret, comedy and musicals in its four theatres. Drop by to see what's on during your stay.

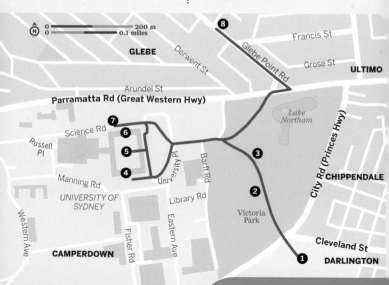

**2 Venture into Victoria Park**

The green gateway to the Inner West and the University of Sydney, **Victoria Park** (cnr Parramatta & City Rds; 🚌422-440) is a 9-hectare grassy wedge revolving around pond-like Lake Northam. In February, 75,000 people descend on the park for the Mardi Gras Fair Day: dog shows, live performances and the 'Miss Fair Day' drag competition.

**3 Dip into Victoria Park Pool**

This 50m heated outdoor **pool** (☎9518 4800; www.cityofsydney.nsw.gov.au; cnr Parramatta & City Rds; adult/child $5.20/3.30; ⏲6am-7pm; 🚌431-440) in Victoria Park serves as Newtown and Glebe's beach. There's also a gym ($15 with pool access), crèche, cafe and swim shop.

**4 Nick into the Nicholson**

The **Nicholson Museum** (☎9351 2812; www.usyd.edu.au; University of Sydney; admission free; ⏲10am-4.30pm Mon-Fri, noon-4pm 1st Sat of month; 🚌422-440) is a must-see for ancient history geeks, with its amazing accumulation of Greek, Roman, Cypriot, Egyptian and Near Eastern antiquities. It was founded in 1860 by orphan-made-good Sir Charles Nicholson, a key figure in the establishment of the university.

**5 Cross the Quadrangle**

Flanked by two grand halls that wouldn't be out of place in Harry Potter's beloved Hogwarts, the Quadrangle has a Gothic Revival design that tips its mortarboard towards the stately colleges of Oxford.

**6 Peruse the University Art Gallery**

Founded at the same time as the university, this **gallery** (admission free; ⏲10am-4.30pm Mon-Fri, noon-4pm 1st Sat of month) has accumulated 2600 works of Aboriginal, Australian, East Asian and European art. Alongside the likes of Goya, Miró and Chagall are a swag of important Australian artists: Sidney Nolan, Arthur Boyd, Grace Cossington Smith, Arthur Streeton, James Gleeson, Margaret Preston, Russell Drysdale, Jeffrey Smart.

**7 Meander through the Macleay**

Nearby, the **Macleay Museum** (admission free; ⏲10am-4.30pm Mon-Fri, noon-4pm 1st Sat of month) has a musty dead smell (old dons or the aged collection of taxidermied Australian fauna?). There's also a historic photography collection, and an early collection of Aboriginal, Torres Strait and Pacific Island cultural material.

**8 Slink into Sappho's Books**

Combining the essentials of student life – books, coffee and alcohol – Sappho's has a bohemian garden **cafe** (☎9552 4498; www.sapphobooks.com.au; 51 Glebe Point Rd; mains $6-18; ⏲8.30am-6.30pm Sun-Tue, 8.30am-11pm Wed-Sat; 🚌Glebe), its walls scrawled with generations of graffiti. The coffee's excellent and the food includes a healthy selection of salads, panini and light breakfasts.

E

Pyrmont Bridge
Cockle Bay
Convention Bay
Darling Dr
Murray St
Harwood St
Experiment St
**Harris St**

Tumbalong Park
Exhibition Centre
Pyrmont St
Pier St
Power House Museum
**16** ✕
**2** Systrum St

Thomas St

White Rabbit
Balfour St
**1**

**ULTIMO**

Bulwarra Rd

Jones St

**Abercrombie St**

**Harris St**

Bulwarra Rd

Quarry St

William Henry St

**Wattle St**

Mountain St

**Broadway**

Knox St

Myrtle St

**CHIPPENDALE**

Bulwarra Rd
Fish Market

**PYRMONT**

Wentworth Park

Wentworth Park

**7**

Bay St

Greek St
Francis St

**25**

**31**

**32**

Grose St

Lake Northam

Victoria Park

Science Rd

Manning Rd

Bank St
Rozelle Bay

Blackwattle Bay

Bellevue St
Darghan St
Darling St
Colbourne Ave
Gottenham St
Talfourd St

Doherty Reserve

Broughton St
Glebe St
Campbell St
Glebe Point Rd
Derwent St
Westmoreland St

**8** ✕

Ferry Rd

Glebe

**GLEBE**

Blackwattle Park
Cook St
Stewart St

Avona Ave

Glebe Point Rd

Allen St

Mansfield St
Avenue Rd
Toxteth Rd
Arcadia Rd
Boyce St

Wigram Rd

Hereford St

Dr HJ Foley Rest Park

St James Reserve

Reuss St
St Johns Rd
Mt Vernon St

Catherine St

Forest Rd

**Ross St**

**FOREST LODGE**

**Bridge Rd**

Pope Paul VI Reserve

Sze Yup Temple
**5**

Edward St

Jubilee Park
**6**

Federal Park

Bicentennial Park

Jubilee & Bicentennial Parks

Jubilee Park

Chapman Rd

Johnstons Creek

Trafalgar St

Nelson St

The Crescent

Lewis Hoad Reserve
Albert St
Charles St

**Minogue Cres**

Hogan Park

Orphan School Creek

Booth St

Taylor St

**Parramatta Rd (Great Western Hwy)**

**Pyrmont Bridge Rd**

Purkis St
Barr St
**17** ✕

D

C

B

A

1

2

3

4

REDFERN

Renwick St

Cope St

Botany Rd

Regent St

Gibbons St

Wyndham St

Garden St

Cleveland St

Lawson St

Redfern

Gerard St

Edward St

Phillips St

Ivy St

DARLINGTON

Lander St

EVELEIGH

Lyne St

Carriageworks
3

Wilson St

Rose St

Abercrombie St

Darlington Rd

Newton St

Dibbs St

Copeland St

Sutter St

Belmont St

Mitchell Rd

Erskineville
Park

Ashmore St

Swanson St

City Rd (Princes Hwy)

Fisher Rd

CAMPERDOWN

Forbes La

Park St

Railway Pde

Foxall Ave

ERSKINEVILLE

UNIVERSITY
OF SYDNEY

Wilson St

Macdonaldtown

Binning St

Western Ave

Carillon Ave

Hollis
Jack Park
Haynes
Reserve

Watkin St

Burren St

Erskineville

20 27

Malcolm St

Bridge St

Royal
Prince Alfred
Hospital

Campbell St

33

Watkin La

Charles St
John St

9

George St

Dunblane St

Missenden Rd

10
13

21 14

22 26

Egan St

Green
Bans
Park

23

Prospect St

Amy St

Hordern St

Church St

29

Linthorpe St

Union St

Gowrie St

Church St

Northwood St

4
Carperdown
Cemetery

30

11

38

Newman St

Newtown

Mallett St

Roberts St

Hopetoun St

19

24 15

12

18

34

35

37

Fowler St

Australia St

Denison St

Probert St

NEWTOWN

King St (Princes Hwy)

9

Norfolk St

Australia St

Ross St

Chelmsford St

Oxford St

Baltic St

36

Enmore Rd

Gladstone St

28

Pemell St

Sloane St

Fulham St

Kent St

Camden St

Alice St

Amy St

For reviews see

Sights        p82
Eating        p84
Drinking      p86
Entertainment p90
Shopping      p90

500 m
0.25 miles

# Sights

## White Rabbit

GALLERY

1 ◉ Map p80, E4

If you're an art lover or a bit of a Mad Hatter, this private collection of cutting-edge, contemporary Chinese art will leave you grinning like a Cheshire Cat. Who knew that the People's Republic was turning out work that was so edgy, funny, sexy or idiosyncratic? (www.whiterabbitcollection.org; 30 Balfour St; admission free; ⏰10am-6pm Thu-Sun; 🚇Redfern)

## Powerhouse Museum

MUSEUM

2 ◉ Map p80, E3

A short walk from Darling Harbour, Sydney's most kid-focused museum whirs away inside the former power station for Sydney's defunct tram network. High-voltage interactive demonstrations wow school groups with the low-down on how lightning strikes, magnets grab and engines growl. Look out for the Strasburg Clock replica on level 3 and the mad scientist experimentation stuff on level 1. (📞9217 0111; www.powerhousemuseum.com; 500 Harris St; adult/child $12/6; ⏰9.30am-5pm; 🚇Paddy's Markets)

## Carriageworks

ARTS CENTRE

3 ◉ Map p80, D6

Built between 1880 and 1889, this intriguing group of huge Victorian-era workshops was part of the Eveleigh Railyards. The rail workers chugged out in 1988 and in 2007 the artists pranced in. It's now home to various avant-garde arts and performance projects, and there's usually something interesting to check out. (📞8571 9111; www.performancespace.com.au; 245 Wilson St; admission free; ⏰10am-6pm; 🚇Redfern)

## Camperdown Cemetery

CEMETERY

4 ◉ Map p80, B6

Take a self guided tour beyond the monstrous 1848 fig tree into this dark, eerily unkempt cemetery next to St Stephens Church. Famous Australians buried here between 1849 and 1942 include Eliza Donnithorne, the inspiration for Miss Havisham in Dickens' *Great Expectations*. Book guided tours via the website. (📞9557 2043;

## Q Local Life

### Chippendale

Tucked between Central station, Surry Hills and the University of Sydney, the tiny suburb of Chippendale is one to watch. The White Rabbit gallery is an early herald of what is likely to become one of Sydney's coolest neighbourhoods, particularly once the Jean Nouvel/Sir Norman Foster–driven Central Park complex of sustainable plant-covered towers and terraces starts to take shape. Meanwhile, Frank Gehry is working on a dramatic crumpled-looking building just across Broadway. Watch this space.

NICK GREEN / GETTY IMAGES ©

Powerhouse Museum

www.ststephens.org.au; 189 Church St; tours $10; ☉sunrise-sunset, tours 11.30am 1st Sun of the month Feb-Dec; 🚊Newtown)

## Sze Yup Temple

TEMPLE

**5** 📍 Map p80, B2

This humble backstreet temple was opened in 1898 by immigrants from the Sze Yup area of China. It's dedicated to 3rd-century folk hero Kwan Ti, whose embroidered, green-robed image takes centre stage on the altar. He is looked to by supplicants as a wise judge, guide and protector. Respectful visitors are welcome; take your shoes off before entering. (📞9660 6465; 2 Edward St; ☉10am-5pm; 🚊Jubilee Park)

## Jubilee & Bicentennial Parks

PARKS

**6** 📍 Map p80, A2

These rolling, grassy parks merge together to offer some tasty views across Rozelle Bay and of both the Anzac and Harbour Bridges. Massive fig and palm trees dot the lawns. A path leads from here along the shoreline to Blackwattle Bay, passing the Victorian Italianate **Bellevue Cottage** (1896) and a park built around the temple-like ruins of an industrial incinerator. (Glebe Point Rd; 🚊Jubilee Park)

## Wentworth Park
GREYHOUND RACING

7   Map p80, D2

Wentworth Park is Australia's premier greyhound-racing complex, where the fast, skinny mutts salivate after tin hares twice weekly. Dog races have been happening here since 1932, and there's a lovely old-fashioned vibe about the place. There are bars and a bistro on site. (☎9552 1799; www.went worthparksport.com.au; Wentworth Park Rd; ⏰Fri & Sat evenings; ☒Wentworth Park)

# Eating

## Eveleigh Farmers' Market
MARKET $

More than 70 regular stallholders sell their goodies at Sydney's best farmers market, held in a heritage-listed railway workshop. Food and coffee stands do a brisk business; celebrity chef Kylie Kwong can often be spotted cooking up a storm. Located at Carriageworks (see 3 ◉ Map p80, D6). (www .eveleighmarket.com.au; Carriageworks, 243 Wilson St; ⏰8am-1pm Sat; ☒Redfern)

## Boathouse on Blackwattle Bay
SEAFOOD $$$

8 ✕  Map p80, C1

The best restaurant in Glebe, and one of the best seafood restaurants in Sydney. Offerings range from oysters so fresh you'd think you shucked them yourself, to a snapper pie that'll go straight to the top of your favourite dish list. Amazing Anzac Bridge views; reservations essential. (☎9518 9011; www.boathouse.net.au; end of Ferry Rd; mains $41-48; ⏰lunch Thu-Sun, dinner Tue-Sun; ☒Glebe)

## Bloodwood
INTERNATIONAL $$

9 ✕  Map p80, B7

Relax over a few drinks and a progression of small plates (we love those polenta chips!) in the front bar, or make your way to the rear to enjoy soundly conceived and expertly cooked dishes from across the globe. The decor is industrial-chic and the vibe is alternative – very Newtown. No bookings. (www.bloodwoodnewtown.com; 416 King St; dishes $7-32; ⏰lunch Fri-Sun, dinner Wed-Mon; ☒Newtown)

## Luxe
CAFE $

10 ✕  Map p80, B6

Campos next door might be the pinnacle of caffeine culture but if you want to sit down, read the paper and eat something more substantial, Luxe is the dux. The menu is limited (a couple of cooked brekky options; pasta or fish for lunch) but the counter of this industrial-chic bakery-cafe is chockfull with chunky sandwiches, moist cakes and delicate tarts. (194 Missenden Rd; breakfast $6-11, lunch $10-16; ⏰breakfast & lunch; ☒Macdonaldtown)

## Vargabar Espresso
CAFE $

11 ✕  Map p80, B7

A diminutive dark-pink cafe with an electric-blue coffee machine, Varga trades on big breakfasts and generates too many hard decisions for 8am. The pesto fried eggs or the breakfast burrito? Both? (☏9517 1932; www .vargabarnewtown.com.au; 10 Wilson St; mains \$10-16; ⊙7am-6pm Mon-Fri, 8am-5.30 Sat & Sun; 🛜; ☒Newtown)

### Black Star Pastry

BAKERY \$

 12 Map p80, B7

Wise people follow the Star to pay homage to excellent coffee, a large selection of sweet things and a few very good savoury things (gourmet pies and the like). There are only a couple of little tables; it's more a snack-and-run or picnic-in-the-park kind of place. (www.blackstarpastry.com .au; 277 Australia St; items \$6-10; ⊙7am-5pm; ☒Newtown)

### Campos

CAFÉ \$

13 Map p80, B6

Trying to squeeze into crowded Campos, king of Sydney's bean scene, can be a challenge. Bean fiends come from miles around – hat-wearing students, broadsheet literati, window-seat daydreamers and doctors on a break from the hospital – all gagging for a shot of 'Campos Superior' blend. (☏9516 3361; www.camposcoffee.com; 193 Missenden Rd; items \$4; ⊙7am-4pm Mon-Sat; ☒Macdonaldtown)

### Thanh Binh

VIETNAMESE \$\$

 14 Map p80, B6

If you're used to Vietnamese restaurants where everything is pre-rolled

and ready to be shovelled straight into your mouth, you haven't really had Vietnamese food. At Thanh Binh playing with your food is part of the fun. Load up your prawn cracker, soak your rice paper, pluck your herbs and launch into a wrapping, rolling, dipping and feasting frenzy. (☏9557 1175; www.thanhbinh.com.au; 111 King St; mains \$14-24; ⊙lunch Wed-Sun, dinner daily; ☒Macdonaldtown)

### Thai Pothong

THAI \$\$

 15 Map p80, B7

This place has won a bowlful of 'Best Thai Restaurant in Sydney' awards. The menu is predictable and the usual crowd of golden Buddhas festoons the walls, but the mood is oddly romantic. Pull up a window seat and watch the Newtowners pass by.

Deus Cafe

(📞9550 6277; www.thaipothong.com.au; 294 King St; mains $15-30; 🕑lunch & dinner; 🗷; 🚃Newtown)

## Mecca Espresso CAFE $

16  Map p80, E3

Mecca has devotees cramming its industrial interior – more for the transcendent coffee than the food, it's fair to say, but there are tasty bites to be had (cooked breakfasts, panini, 'roast on a roll'). (www.meccaespresso.com.au; 646 Harris St; mains $7-11; 🕑breakfast & lunch Mon-Sat; 🚃Central)

## Deus Cafe CAFE $$

17  Map p80, B4

Strewn with vintage motorcycles and kooky two-wheelin' art, Deus Cafe is an extension of an eccentric motorbike shop on frenzied Parramatta Rd. Start the day with a classic: a Triumph Bonneville T100 or a ham-and-cheese croissant with a high-revving coffee. Hearty mains (burgers, steak sandwiches, pasta) kick in as the day progresses. (📞9519 3669; 98-104 Parramatta Rd; breakfast & lunch $8-17, dinner $18-25; 🕑breakfast & lunch daily, dinner Wed-Sun; 🚌436-440)

# Drinking

## Bank Hotel PUB, DJ

18  Map p80, B7

There's been bags of cash splashed about the Bank, but it still attracts a kooky mix of lesbians (especially for

Lady L on Wednesdays), students, sports fans, gay guys and just about everyone else – they just don't wear their Ugg boots to the pub anymore. The portfolio includes a rooftop terrace, cocktail bar, Thai restaurant and DJs. (☑8568 1900; www.bankhotel.com.au; 324 King St; ⊙10am-late; ☒Newtown)

## Courthouse Hotel PUB

19 Map p80, A7

What a brilliant pub! A block back from the King St fray, the 150-year-old Courthouse is the kind of place where everyone from pool-playing goth lesbians to magistrates can have a beer and feel right at home. How ironic – the complete absence of social judgement in a pub called the Courthouse. Beer specials and good pub grub, too. (☑9519 8273; 202 Australia St; ⊙10am-midnight Mon-Sat, to 10pm Sun; ☒Newtown)

## Hive BAR

20 Map p80, C7

In increasingly groovy Erskineville village, this breezy little corner bar lures the neighbourhood's hipsters with excellent food, cocktails, DJs spinning funk and soul, crazy murals and a quiet bolthole upstairs. Order a few plates to share over a glass of vino and pull up a footpath table. (☑9519 9911; www.thehivebar.com.au; 93 Erskineville Rd; ⊙11.30am-midnight Mon-Fri, 8am-midnight Sat & Sun; ☒Erskineville)

Local Life
## Live Music at Pubs

At the forefront of Sydney's live music scene, the **Annandale Hotel** (Map p80, A5; ☑9550 1078; www.annandalehotel.com; 17 Parramatta Rd; admission free-$28; ☐436-440) coughs up alt-rock, metal, punk and electronica. Minimal (or no) cash will score you a live-music fix (everything from acoustic to goth) at the **Sandringham Hotel** (Map p80, A7; ☑9557 1254; www.sando.com.au; 387 King St; admission free-$35; 🛜; ☒Newtown), where, according to local band The Whitlams, God sometimes drops by. Intimate 1920s-themed **Vanguard** (Map p80, C6; ☑9557 7992; www.thevanguard.com.au; 42 King St; dinner & show $51-82, general admission $16-32; ☒Macdonaldtown) stages live music most nights, as well as burlesque, comedy and movie screenings.

## Jester Seeds COCKTAIL BAR

21 Map p80, B6

Jester Seeds is very Newtown. By that we mean a bit gloomy, a little grungy and very hip, with the requisite mismatched furniture, graffiti, obtuse name, astroturf 'garden' and a classic but credible soundtrack. And the cocktails are great. (www.jesterseeds.com; 127 King St; ⊙4pm-midnight Tue-Sat, 4-10pm Sun; ☒Macdonaldtown)

## Corridor
COCKTAIL BAR

**22** 🍷 Map p80, B6

The name exaggerates this bar's skinniness, but not by much. Downstairs the bartenders serve old-fashioned cocktails and a good range of wine, while upstairs there's art for sale and a tiny deck. (www.corridorbar.com.au; 153a King St; ⏰3pm-midnight Tue-Fri, 1pm-midnight Sat, 1-10pm Sun; 🚇Macdonaldtown)

## Imperial Hotel
GAY, CLUB

**23** 🍷 Map p80, B7

The art deco Imperial is legendary as the setting for *The Adventures of Priscilla, Queen of the Desert*. The front bar is a lively place for poolshooting and cruising, with the action shifting to the cellar club late on a Saturday night. But it's in the cabaret bar that the legacy of Priscilla is kept alive. (www.theimperialhotel.com.au; 35 Erskineville Rd; front bar free, cellar club before/after 10pm free/$10, cabaret bar Fri/Sat $10/15; ⏰3pm-late; 🚇Erskineville)

## Zanzibar
BAR

**24** 🍷 Map p80, B7

Eastern opulence continues all the way to the roof at this late-night Newtown bar behind a winged art deco facade. Catch the sunset from the rooftop, settle into a cushioned couch or shoot some pool in the funky downstairs bar. Beaut bar food; $8 cocktails until 10pm. (☎9519 1511; www.zanzibarnewtown.com.au; 323 King St; ⏰10am-5am Mon-Sat, to midnight Sun; 🚇Newtown)

## Friend In Hand Hotel
PUB

**25** 🍷 Map p80, D3

At heart Friend In Hand is still a working class pub with a resident loud-mouth cockatoo and a cast of grizzly old timers and local larrikins propping up the bar. But then there's all the other stuff: life drawing, poetry readings, crab racing, comedy nights. Strewth Beryl, bet you weren't expecting that. (☎9660 2326; www.friendinhand.com.au; 58 Cowper St; ⏰8am-midnight Mon-Sat, 10am-10pm Sun; 🚌Glebe)

## Marlborough Hotel
PUB

**26** 🍷 Map p80, B6

A straighter version of the Bank, the Marly has a front sports bar with live bands on weekends, a shady beer garden, a cellar nightclub and a large cocktail floor with a cool wraparound terrace. (☎9519 1222; www.marlboroughhotel.com.au; 145 King St; ⏰10am-late Mon-Sat, noon-late Sun; 🚇Macdonaldtown)

## Rose of Australia
PUB

**27** 🍷 Map p80, C7

The aubergine and umber renovations to this gorgeous old corner pub haven't dented the tiled front bar's charm one iota. Locals of all persuasions hang out here, catching some afternoon rays at the street-side tables, a footy game on the big screens or a meal upstairs. Live bands Fridays. (☎9565 1441; www.roseofaustralia.com.au; 1 Swanson St; ⏰10am-11pm; 🚇Erskineville)

Understand
## Sydney's Music Scene

### Rock & Alternative

In the 1970s and '80s Australia churned out a swag of iconic pub rockers, with Sydney bands INXS and Midnight Oil at the forefront. During the '90s and noughties, when guitar bands came back into vogue, contrary Sydney popped a pill and headed to the disco. Most of the significant Australian acts of the era formed elsewhere, with the exception of garage rockers the Vines and the Cops, cartoon punks Frenzal Rhomb, singer-songwriter Alex Lloyd and jangly sentimentalists the Whitlams. In the meantime, Sydney's most successful musical export was children's novelty act The Wiggles.

Things have been looking up in recent years, with the city turning out the likes of electro popsters the Presets, hard rockers Wolfmother, folky siblings Angus & Julia Stone, alternative rock lads Boy & Bear and indie disco kids the Jezabels.

### Pop & Dance

Australia loves its pop stars and dance divas, and is currently churning them out at a rate of knots in reality TV shows. While most inevitably sink without a trace, Sydneysiders Guy Sebastian and Altiyan Childs have gone on to have considerable hits. Others have taken the more traditional route to pop stardom: starring in a cheesy soap opera. Melbourne can lay claim to Kylie, but Sydney makes do with Delta Goodrem and Natalie Imbruglia.

Sydney loves to cut a rug, and you'll find a bit of everything being played around the dance clubs, from drum and bass to electro. Homegrown dance music is made by the likes of Bag Raiders and Art vs Science, and spun by popular DJs such as Tom Piper, Timmy Trumpet, Kid Kenobi and Ajax.

### Opera

With an opera house as its very symbol, no discussion of Sydney's musical legacy is complete without mentioning Dame Joan Sutherland (1926–2010), the Eastern Beaches lass who became one of the greatest opera singers of the 20th century. Her legacy can be seen in the success of Opera Australia and singers such as Cheryl Barker.

Gleebooks

# Entertainment

### Enmore Theatre    PERFORMING ARTS

28  Map p80, A7

Originally a vaudeville playhouse, the elegantly wasted, 2500-capacity Enmore now hosts such acts as Queens of the Stone Age, Wilco and PJ Harvey, plus theatre and comedy. Cafe, wooden floors, lounge areas and balconies. (📞9550 3666; www.enmore theatre.com.au; 130 Enmore Rd; tickets $18-79; 🕓box office 9am-6pm Mon-Fri, 10am-2pm Sat; 🚆Newtown)

### Performance Space    PERFORMING ARTS

This edgy artists' hub that is situated at the Carriageworks arts centre (see 3 ◉ Map p80, D6) stages performances of new dance, acrobatic and multimedia works – basically anything that can be lumped under the broad umbrella of 'the arts'. (📞8571 9111; www .performancespace.com.au; Carriageworks, 245 Wilson St; tickets adult/concession $30/20; 🚆Redfern)

### Dendy Newtown    CINEMA

29  Map p80, B6

Follow the buttery scent of popcorn into the dark folds of this plush cinema, screening first-run, independent world films. (📞9550 5699; www.dendy .com.au; 261 King St; adult/child $17/12; 🚆Newtown)

# Shopping

### Better Read Than Dead    BOOKS

30 🔒 Map p80, B6

This just might be our favourite Sydney bookshop, and not just because of the pithy name and great selection of Lonely Planet titles. Nobody seems to mind if you waste hours perusing the beautifully presented aisles, stacked with high-, medium- and deliciously low-brow reading materials. (📞9557 8700; www.betterread.com.au; 265 King St; 🕓9.30am-9pm; 🚆Newtown)

## Gleebooks BOOKS

**31** Map p80, D4

Gleebooks is regarded by many to be Sydney's best bookshop. The aisles are packed with politics, arts and general fiction, and staff really know their stuff. Check its calendar for author talks and book launches. (9660 2333; www.glee books.com.au; 49 Glebe Point Rd; 9am-7pm Sun-Wed, 9am-9pm Thu-Sat; Glebe)

## Glebe Markets MARKETS

**32** Map p80, D4

The best of the west; Sydney's dread-locked, shoeless, inner-city contingent beats a course to this crowded hippy-ish market. (www.glebemarkets.com.au; Glebe Public School, cnr Glebe Point Rd & Derby Pl; 10am-4pm Sat; Glebe)

## Gould's Book Arcade BOOKS

**33** Map p80, C6

Possibly the world's scariest second-hand bookstore, the floor-to-ceiling racks and stacks seem in perpetual danger of burying you under a tonne of Stalinist analysis. All manner of musty out-of-print books are stocked, with the owner's leftie leanings displayed along one very large wall. Cassettes, records and old video tapes, too (VHS and Beta!). (9519 8947; www .gouldsbooks.com; 32 King St; 10am-10pm; Macdonaldtown)

---

## Understand
### Literary Sydney

Australia's literary history harks back to Sydney's convict days. New experiences and landscapes inspired the colonists to commit their stories to the page. Though many early works have been lost, some – like Marcus Clarke's *For the Term of His Natural Life* (1870) – have become legendary.

By the late 19th century, a more formal Australian literary movement was developing with *The Bulletin,* an influential magazine promoting egalitarian and unionist thinking. Well-known contributing authors of the time included Henry Lawson (1867–1922) and AB 'Banjo' Paterson (1864–1941), who penned *Waltzing Matilda*.

*My Brilliant Career* (1901) by Miles Franklin (1879–1954), is considered the first authentic Australian novel. The book caused a sensation when it was revealed that Miles was actually a woman.

Multi-award-winning Sydney authors of international stature include Patrick White (Nobel Prize in Literature 1973), Thomas Keneally (Booker Prize winner 1982), Peter Carey (Booker Prize winner 1988 and 2001) and Kate Grenville (Commonwealth Writers' Prize winner 2006). Other authors of note include David Malouf, Mandy Sayer, Shirley Hazzard, Eleanor Dark and Ruth Park.

Deus Ex Machina

### Eveleigh Artisans' Market
MARKET

A monthly forum for contemporary artisans and designers in various fields to sell their treasures directly to the public. Located at Carriageworks (see 3 ⊙ Map p80, D6). (www.eveleighmarket.com.au; Carriageworks, 243 Wilson St; ⊙10am-3pm 1st Sun of the month; 🚉Redfern)

### Faster Pussycat
CLOTHING, ACCESSORIES

**34** 🔒 Map p80, A8

Inspired by 'trash pop culture, hot rods and rock and roll', this cool cat coughs up clothing and accessories for all genders and ages (including baby punkwear) in several shades of Newtown black. (📞9519 1744; www.

fasterpussycatonline.com; 431a King St; ⊙11am-6pm; 🚉Newtown)

### Deus Ex Machina
CLOTHING, ACCESSORIES

Translating to 'God is in the machine', this kooky showroom is crammed with classic and custom-made motorcycles and surfboards. This is 'postmodern motorcyclism' – a hybrid workshop, cafe and offbeat boutique, with men's and women's threads, including Deus-branded jeans, tees and shorts. Located at Deus cafe (see 17 ✖ Map p80, B4). (📞8594 2800; http://au.deuscustoms.com; 98-104 Parramatta Rd; ⊙9am-5pm; 🚌436-440)

## Newtown Old Wares ANTIQUES

**35** 🔒 Map p80, A8

Yearning for a vintage Cilla Black poster, a safari suit or a Blaxploitation lamp? This funky antiques store covers the cool and the kitsch from 'deco to disco': old transistor radios, TVs, telephones, jukeboxes, barstools, vinyl couches...perfect for pottering about. (☎9519 6705; 439 King St; ⏰10am-5pm Tue-Sun; ⓡNewtown)

## Le Cabinet des Curiosities CLOTHING, MUSIC

**36** 🔒 Map p80, A7

Enter, if you dare, into a dark world of black metal, goth, paganism and the occult and depart, if you're able, laden with chunky jewellery, skull-encrusted platform boots, scarlet and black corsets, and a copy of *Gothic Beauty* magazine. (www.curiosities.com.au; 97 Enmore Rd; ⏰11am-6pm Tue, Wed & Fri-Sun, 11am-8pm Thu; ⓡNewtown)

## Frolic CLOTHING, ACCESSORIES

**37** 🔒 Map p80, B8

Funky tees, sunnies, hats, vintage dresses – frisky Frolic specialises in 1950s to 1980s secondhand men's and women's clothes, as well as stocking several local brands. Masquerade as a local with a Newtown Jets T-shirt. (☎9519 9895; 461 King St; ⏰11am-6pm Wed-Mon, 11am-3.30pm Tue; ⓡNewtown)

## Egg Records MUSIC

**38** 🔒 Map p80, B7

There's something a bit too cool about this secondhand and new music store, but it's the perfect place to, say, complete your collection of 1980s David Bowie 12-inch singles, or pick up a Cramps T-shirt or a Gene Simmons figurine. (☎9550 6056; www.eggrecords online.com; 3 Wilson St; ⏰10am-6.30pm Mon-Sat, 11am-5pm Sun; ⓡNewtown)

Explore

# Surry Hills & Darlinghurst

Sydney's hippest and gayest neighbourhood is also home to its most interesting dining and bar scene. For the most part it's more gritty than pretty, and actual sights are thin on the ground, but there's still plenty to do and see here, especially after dark. Rows of Victorian terrace houses are a reminder of its working class roots.

# The Sights in a Day

☀ Spend most of the morning wandering around the **Australian Museum** (p96) and then take a long, leisurely walk to lunch at **House** (p103). To get there, follow the edge of Hyde Park along College St, continue down Wentworth and then veer left on to Elizabeth.

☀ After lunch, head along to Albion St and turn left to wander through the heart of Surry Hills. Turn left on Bourke St to check out **Object Gallery** (p100) within the old St Margaret's Hospital complex. Head up to Taylor Square, the hub of gay community life, and cross into Darlinghurst. Take Forbes St and cut through the **National Art School** (p100), stopping for a quick look around the gallery. Exiting on Burton St, turn right and continue to **Green Park** (p102). Spend the rest of the afternoon exploring the **Sydney Jewish Museum** (p100).

☾ Head out early and catch a cab to **Porteño** (p102); they don't take bookings, so you might have to spend some time propping up the bar. After dinner, if you haven't booked tickets for a play at **Belvoir St Theatre** (p106) or a gig at the **Gaelic Club** (p108), take a stroll along Crown St. There are plenty of good bars and pubs to inspect along the way.

 **Top Sights**

Australian Museum (p96)

♥ **Best of Sydney**

**Eating**

Porteño (p102)

Universal (p103)

Longrain (p103)

Bar H (p103)

House (p103)

**Drinking**

Pocket (p104)

Hinky Dinks (p105)

Shady Pines Saloon (p105)

Beresford Hotel (p105)

**Gay & Lesbian**

Oxford Hotel (p105)

## Getting There

🚆 **Train** Apart from the very eastern fringe of Surry Hills, a train station is never more than a kilometre away. Exit at Museum for the blocks around Oxford St; Central for the rest of Surry Hills; and Kings Cross for the northern reaches of Darlinghurst.

🚌 **Bus** Numerous buses traverse Cleveland, Crown, Albion, Oxford, Liverpool and Flinders Sts.

## Top Sights
# Australian Museum

This natural history museum, established just 40 years after the First Fleet dropped anchor, has endeavoured to shrug off its museum-that-should-be-in-a-museum feel by jazzing things up a little. Hence dusty taxidermy has been interspersed with video projections and a terrarium with live snakes, while dinosaur skeletons cosy up to life-size recreations. Yet it's the most old-fashioned section that is arguably the most interesting – the hall of bones and the large collection of crystals and precious stones.

Map p98, B1

☏9320 6000

www.amonline.net.au

6 College St

adult/child/family $12/6/30

⏱9.30am-5pm

⛫Museum

Australian Museum

# Don't Miss

### Surviving Australia

Exhibits simultaneously play up to tourists fears of dangerous critters while cleverly contrasting this with information on animal extinctions. There are interesting displays on extinct megafauna such as the marsupial lion and giant wombat (simultaneously cuddly and terrifying). A sad 'where are they now' exhibit features stuffed remains and video footage of recently extinct species such as the Tasmanian tiger.

### Indigenous Australians

This section covers Aboriginal history and spirituality, from Dreamtime stories to the Freedom Rides of the 1960s, to contemporary issues – making good use of historic video clips and recorded testimonies along the way. A jail cell has a sobering account of Aboriginal deaths in custody, while political posters trace the history of the long battle for indigenous rights.

### Skeletons

The fabulously macabre hall of bones, near the main entrance, has an intriguingly bizarre tableau of a skeletal man riding a horse. On the other wall, Skeletor sits in a comfy chair with his underfed dog and a bird in a cage, while his cat chases a rat. Another bony bro has been made to look like it's riding a bicycle.

### Minerals

In neighbouring halls on the first level, the Planet of Minerals and the Chapman Mineral Collection house a fascinating array of colourful, glittering and implausibly shaped things that have been dug out of the earth and collected from caves. Check out the giant casts of actual gold nuggets found in Australia.

☑ **Top Tips**

▶ Special temporary exhibitions are held regularly and are charged separately.

▶ You can leave and re-enter the museum; pop out for a picnic in Hyde Park.

▶ Children under five get in for free.

▶ Kidspace on level two is a mini-museum for the under-fives.

✗ **Take a Break**

Just down the hill from the museum, **Bar Reggio** (Map p98, C1; ☎9332 1129; www.barreggio.com.au; 135 Crown St; mains $12-25; ⏱lunch & dinner Mon-Sat; 🚇Museum) is a remnant of a tiny Italian enclave centred on Stanley St. Its pasta, pizza and grills have stood the test of time.

The museum has its own cafe, located on the ground floor near the entrance.

Moore Park Rd
Greens Rd
Iris St
Selwyn St
Josephson St
Kippax Lagoon
Gregory Ave
MOORE PARK
Anzac Pde
Sydney Boys & Girls High Schools
Flinders St
Hutchinson St
Nichols St
Fitzroy St ⊜ 20
Bennett St
Prospect St
Fred Miller Park
Phelps St
Arthur St
Nobbs St
Moore Park
South Dowling St
Cleveland St
32 ⊜
400 m
0.25 miles
Fitzroy Pl
Fitzroy St
29 ⊜
Collins La
Rainford St
Davies St
Raper St
Brett Whiteley Studio 3 ⊚
Markham St
Mort St
Ridge St
Chelsea St
Nickson St
Wilchire St
Bourke St
12 ⊗
Norton St
Griffin St
Arthur St
Tudor St
Crown St
Baptist St
SURRY HILLS
Riley St
Foveaux St
13 ⊜
Waterloo St
Lacey St
Little Riley St
Adelaide St
Ward Park
Marlborough St
Riley St
Goodlet St
Goodlet La
7 ⊗
Cleveland St
Cleveland St
⊙ N
Sophia St
Kippax St
Cooper St
Hart St
Holt St
Devonshire St
Belvoir St
Wilton St
James St
Elizabeth St
27 ⊚
Randle St
Chalmers St
Chalmers La
Buckingham St
Cisdell St
25 ⊚
Great Buckingham St
Buckingham St

**For reviews see**

| ⊙ | Top Sights | p96 |
| ⊚ | Sights | p100 |
| ⊗ | Eating | p102 |
| ⊕ | Drinking | p104 |
| ⊕ | Entertainment | p106 |
| ⊜ | Shopping | p108 |

# Sights

## Sydney Jewish Museum  MUSEUM

1 ⊙ Map p98, D3

Created as a living memorial to the Holocaust, the Sydney Jewish Museum examines Australian Jewish history, culture and tradition from the time of the First Fleet (which included 16 known Jews) to the present day, along with the history of Judaism in general. Video testimony and touch-screen computers are used to good effect. (☎9360 7999; www.sydney jewishmuseum.com.au; 148 Darlinghurst Rd; adult/child/family $10/6/22; ⏰10am-4pm Sun-Thu, to 2pm Fri; ◪Kings Cross)

CLAVER CARROLL / GETTY IMAGES ©

Brett Whiteley Studio, *Unfinished Beach Polyptych* (detail), Brett Whiteley © Wendy Whiteley

## National Art School  HISTORIC BUILDING, GALLERY

2 ⊙ Map p98, D3

From 1841 to 1912 these bizarre sandstone buildings comprised Darlinghurst Gaol: writer Henry Lawson was incarcerated here several times for debt (he called the place 'Starvinghurst'). If today's art students think they've got it tough, they should spare a thought for the 732 prisoners who were crammed in here, or the 76 who hanged. Visit the excellent students' gallery. (☎9337 8744; www.nas.edu.au; Forbes St; admission free; ⏰10am-4pm Mon-Sat; ◪Kings Cross)

## Brett Whiteley Studio  GALLERY

3 ⊙ Map p98, C6

Whiteley (1939–92) lived fast and without restraint, and when he let fly on the canvas, people sat up and took notice. His hard-to-find studio (look for the signs on Devonshire St) has been preserved as a gallery for some of his best work. At the door is a miniature version of his famous sculpture *Almost Once*. (☎9225 1881; www.brettwhiteley.org; 2 Raper St; admission free; ⏰10am-4pm Fri-Sun; ◪Central)

## Object Gallery  GALLERY

4 ⊙ Map p98, C4

Inside the cylindrical former St Margaret's Hospital chapel (a 1958 modernist classic by architect Ken Woolley), nonprofit Object presents innovative exhibitions of new craft and design from Australia and overseas. Furniture, fashion, textiles and glass festoon three levels. (☎9361 4511; www.object.com.au;

## Understand
## Aboriginal Australia

### Origins & Culture

Australian Aboriginal society has the longest continuous cultural history in the world, its origins dating back to at least the last ice age. Mystery shrouds many aspects of Australian prehistory, but it's thought that the first humans probably came here from Southeast Asia more than 50,000 years ago.

Aborigines were traditionally tribal people, living in extended family groups. Knowledge obtained over millennia enabled them to use their environment extensively and sustainably; intimate knowledge of animal behaviour and plant harvesting ensured food shortages were rare.

The simplicity of Aboriginal technology contrasted with a sophisticated cultural life. Religion, history, law and art were integrated in complex ceremonies.

### Aboriginal Sydney

Governor Arthur Phillip estimated that around 1500 Aborigines lived around Sydney at first contact. The local people were known as the Eora (which literally means 'from this place'), broken into three main language groups and smaller clans such as the Cadigal and the Wangal.

### Dispossession

As Aboriginal society was based on tribal family groups, a coordinated response to the European colonisers wasn't possible. The British declared Australia to be terra nullius (meaning 'land belonging to no one') and claimed it as their own. Some Aborigines were driven away, some were killed, many were shifted onto government reserves and missions, and thousands, including almost all of the Cadigal, succumbed to foreign diseases introduced by the Europeans.

From 1910 to the end of the 1960s, a policy of 'cultural assimilation' allowed Aboriginal children to be forcibly removed from their families and schooled in the ways of white society. Around 100,000 children (dubbed the 'stolen generation') were separated from their parents in this way.

In 1967 a national referendum was held on whether to allow Aboriginal people the right to vote, which was passed by 90% of eligible voters.

## Understand
### Sydney Mardi Gras

Sydney's famous **Mardi Gras** (www.mardigras.org.au) is now the biggest annual tourist-attracting date on the Australian calendar. While the straights focus on the parade, the gay and lesbian community throws itself wholeheartedly into the entire festival, including the blitzkrieg of partying that surrounds it. There's no better time for the gay traveller to visit Sydney than the three-week lead-up to the parade and party, held on the first Saturday in March.

On the big night itself, the parade kicks off around sunset, preceded by the throbbing engines of hundreds of Dykes on Bikes. Heading up Oxford St from Hyde Park, it veers right into Flinders St, hooking into Moore Park Rd and culminating outside the party site in Driver Ave. The whole thing takes about 90 minutes to trundle through, and attracts hundreds of thousands of spectators ogling from the sidelines.

The parade has a serious political bent, commemorating a 1978 gay rights march which ended in participants being arrested and beaten.

415 Bourke St; admission free; ⊙11am-5pm Tue-Fri, 10am-5pm Sat; 🚈Central)

### Green Park                    PARK

5  Map p98, D3

Once the residence of Alexander Green, hangman of Darlinghurst Gaol, Green Park is a cheery space during the day but, as the many syringe-disposal bins attest, it's best avoided at night. At the top of the slope, the inverted pink triangular prism backed by black pillars is the Gay & Lesbian Holocaust Memorial, founded by Auschwitz survivor, Dr Kitty Fischer. (cnr Victoria & Burton Sts; 🚈Kings Cross)

### St John's Church              CHURCH

6  Map p98, E2

Grab a pamphlet inside this lovely sandstone church (1858) for an inter-esting 10-minute, self-guided tour. It makes for a hushed escape from the urban jangle of Darlinghurst Rd and the car wash next door. The Anglican congregation runs the Rough Edges Community Centre, working with the area's many homeless. (☎9360 6844; www.stjohnsanglican.org.au; 120 Darlinghurst Rd; ⊙10am-2.30pm Mon, Tue & Thu-Sat; 🚈Kings Cross)

## Eating

### Porteño                    ARGENTINIAN $$

7 🍴 Map p98, B7

The hip lads who made their mark with Bodega have stepped up their robust homage to the foods of South America, and they've taken loads of fans along for the gastronomically wild ride. Bring a huge appetite and a posse; you can only book for five or more. Don't miss the magnificent eight-hour wood-fired suckling pig. (☎ 8399 1440; www.porteno.com.au; 358 Cleveland St; sharing plates $12-44; ⊙ dinner Mon-Sat; 🚇 Central)

## Universal

FUSION $$

8  Map p98, C2

Simple decor and dramatic lighting set the scene for food which is certainly dramatic and anything but simple. Celebrity chef Christine Manfield's latest venture tours the cuisines of the known universe and creates something out of this world. Dishes are designed to be shared, and the smutty-sounding cocktails shouldn't be missed. (☎ 9331 0709; www.universalrestaurant.com; courtyard, 248 Palmer St; dishes $27-31; ⊙ lunch Fri, dinner Mon-Sat; 🚇 Museum)

## Longrain

THAI $$$

9  Map p98, B3

Inside a century-old, wedge-shaped printing-press building, urbanites slurp down Longrain's signature modern Thai specialities, such as pork-and-prawn-filled eggnet or caramelised pork hock with five spices and chilli vinegar. Sip a Thai-inflected cocktail at the bar afterwards. (☎ 9280 2888; www.longrain.com; 85 Commonwealth St; lunch $27-48, dinner $31-44; ⊙ lunch Fri, dinner daily; 🚇 Central)

## Bar H

CHINESE $$

10  Map p98, B3

It might sound like a medicinal product but banish that thought from your mind as you slink into this sexy, shiny, black-walled corner eatery. Also banish thoughts of ho-hum yum cha, as the pork buns and wontons served here are a complete revelation. Larger dishes – pork belly, steamed fish and roast duck – are just as good. (☎ 9280 1980; www.barhsurryhills.com; 80 Campbell St; dishes $10-36; ⊙ dinner Tue-Sun; 🚇 Museum)

## House

THAI $

11  Map p98, A3

On a sticky Sydney night, House's lantern-strung courtyard really feels like Southeast Asia, not least because of the constant traffic passing and the chicken embryo on the menu. Specialising in the street food of the Issan region of northeast Thailand, the food is deliciously authentic. When they say something is spicy, believe them. (☎ 9280 0364; www.house thai.com.au; 202 Elizabeth St; mains $10-18; ⊙ 11.30am-late; 🚇 Central)

## Marque

MODERN AUSTRALIAN $$$

12  Map p98, C5

It's Mark Best's delicious, inventive, beautifully presented food that has won Marque various best restaurant gongs in recent years; it's certainly not the somewhat stuffy ambience or insipid decor. There's

RICHARD KENDALL / GETTY IMAGES ©

Sydney Mardi Gras

an excellent-value, three-course set lunch on Fridays ($45). (☑9332 2225; www.marquerestaurant.com.au; 355 Crown St; 5/8 courses $95/150; ☺lunch Fri, dinner Mon-Sat; ℝCentral)

### Le Monde                        CAFE $

13 🍴 Map p98, B5

Some of Sydney's best breakfasts are served among the demure dark wooden walls of this small cafe. Top-notch coffee and a terrific selection of tea will gear you up to face the world. (www.lemondecafe.com.au; 83 Foveaux St; mains $9-16; ☺breakfast & lunch Mon-Sat; ℝCentral)

### Single Origin Roasters       CAFE $

14 🍴 Map p98, A3

These impassioned, bouncing-off-the-walls caffeine fiends love to chat about the fair-trade or environmental credentials of their beans. The menu's full of cutely described yummies such as the 'salad of weeds', 'mains and scratchies' and the 'fish finger sarnie innit'. Unshaven graphic artists roll cigarettes at the little outdoor tables in the bricky Chicago-esque hollows of deepest Surry Hills. (☑9211 0665; www.singleorigin.com.au; 60-64 Reservoir St; mains $11-16; ☺6.30am-4pm Mon-Fri; ℝCentral)

### Bentley Restaurant
### & Bar              MODERN AUSTRALIAN $$$

15 🍴 Map p98, C3

The reincarnation of this old corner pub as an upmarket restaurant hasn't thrown the bar out with the bath water. You can still just drop by to sample from the extensive wine list, or settle in for the beautifully presented food at the highly regarded restaurant. Portions are small but inventiveness is high. (☑9332 2344; www.thebentley.com.au; 320 Crown St; mains $33-40; ☺lunch & dinner Tue-Sat; ℝMuseum)

# Drinking

### Pocket                          BAR

16 🍷 Map p98, C2

Sink into the corner Pocket's comfy leather couches, order a drink from one of the cheery waitstaff and chat about the day's adventures accompanied by a decade-defying indie soundtrack. Pop-art murals and exposed brickwork add to the comfortably underground ambience. (www.pocketsydney.com.au; 13 Burton St; ⏱4pm-midnight; ®Museum)

### Hinky Dinks    COCKTAIL BAR

**17**  Map p98, E1

Everything's just hunky dory in this little cocktail bar styled after a 1950s milkshake parlour. Try the Hinky Fizz, an alcohol-soaked strawberry sorbet served in a waxed-paper sundae cup. (www.hinkydinks.com.au; 185 Darlinghurst Rd; ⏱5pm-midnight Mon-Sat; ®Kings Cross)

### Shady Pines Saloon    BAR

**18**  Map p98, C3

With no sign or street number on the door and an entry from a shady back lane (look for the white door before Bikram Yoga on Foley St), this subterranean honky-tonk bar caters to the urban boho in the know. Sip whisky and rye with the good ol' hipster boys amid Western memorabilia and taxidermy. (www.shadypinessaloon.com; shop 4, 256 Crown St; ⏱4pm-midnight; ®Museum)

### Beresford Hotel    PUB, LIVE MUSIC

**19**  Map p98, C4

The once grungy Beresford (circa 1870) has transformed into a superslick architectural tractor beam designed to lure the beautiful people. And it works! The crowd will make

you feel either inadequate or right at home, depending on how the mirror is treating you. Out the back there's a vast new beer garden, while upstairs is a schmick live music/club space. (☏9357 1111; www.theberesford.com.au; 354 Bourke St; ⏱noon-1am; ®Central)

### Cricketers Arms Hotel    PUB

**20**  Map p98, D5

The Cricketers, with its cosy vibe, is a favourite haunt of arts students, turntable fans and locals of all persuasions. It's ace for a beer any time, and there

---

**Q Local Life**

### Darlinghurst's Gay Scene

For 30 years the **Oxford Hotel** (Map p98, D3; ☏8324 5200; www.theoxfordhotel.com.au; 134 Oxford St; ⏱10am-late; ®Museum) has remained the locus of beer-swilling gay blokedom. **Midnight Shift** (Map p98, C3; ☏9358 3848; www.themidnightshift.com.au; 85 Oxford St; admission free-$10; ⏱noon-2am Mon & Tue, noon-4am Wed, Thu & Sun, noon-6am Fri & Sat; ®Museum) is equal parts video bar and nightclub. In subterranean **Palms on Oxford** (Map p98, C3; ☏9357 4166; 124 Oxford St; admission free; ⏱8pm-1am Thu & Sun, to 3am Fri & Sat; ®Museum), the heyday of Stock Aitken Waterman lives on. Serious clubbers head to **Arq** (Map p98, D4; ☏9380 8700; www.arqsydney.com.au; 16 Flinders St; admission free-$25; ⏱9pm-late Thu-Sun; ®Museum).

are open fires for when you need warming up. (📞9331 3301; 106 Fitzroy St; 🚆339)

## The Winery
WINE BAR

**21** 🍷 Map p98, C4

Set back from the road in the shady grounds of a historic water reservoir, this wine bar serves up dozens of wines by the glass to the swankier sector of the Surry Hills hip. Sit here for a while and you'll notice all kinds of kitsch touches lurking in the greenery: garden gnomes, upside-down parrots, iron koalas – or is that the wine speaking? (www.thewinerysurry hills.com.au; 285a Crown St; 🕐noon-midnight; 🚆Museum)

## Victoria Room
COCKTAIL BAR

**22** 🍸 Map p98, E2

Plush chesterfields, art nouveau wallpaper, dark-wood panelling and bamboo screens – the Victoria Room is the spoilt love child of a 1920s Bombay gin palace and a Hong Kong opium den. Don your white linen suit and panama and order a Raspberry Debonair at the bar. (📞9357 4488; www .thevictoriaroom.com; Level 1, 235 Victoria St; 🕐6pm-midnight Tue-Thu, 5pm-2am Fri, noon-2am Sat, noon-midnight Sun; 🚆Kings Cross)

## Oxford Art Factory
BAR, LIVE MUSIC

**23** 🍷 Map p98, C2

The indie kids party against an arty backdrop at this two-room multi-purpose venue modelled on Warhol's New York creative base. There's a gallery, bar and performance space that often hosts international acts and DJs. Check the website for what's on. (www .oxfordartfactory.com; 38-46 Oxford St; cover charge & opening hours vary; 🚆Museum)

## Tio's Cerveceria
BAR

**24** 🍷 Map p98, B3

Tio loves tequila. Heaps of different types. And wrestling, Catholic kitsch and Day of the Dead paraphernalia. Surry Hills skaters, beard-wearers and babydoll babes love him right back. (4-14 Foster St; 🕐4pm-midnight Mon-Sat, 2-10pm Sun; 🚆Museum)

# Entertainment

## Belvoir St Theatre
THEATRE

**25** ⭐ Map p98, A6

In a quiet corner of Surry Hills, this intimate venue hosts the often-experimental and consistently excellent Company B. Shows sometimes feature big stars, such as Geoffrey Rush. (📞9699 3444; www.belvoir.com.au; 25 Belvoir St; tickets $42-62; 🚆Central)

## SBW Stables Theatre
THEATRE

**26** ⭐ Map p98, E2

In the 19th century this place was knee-high in horse dung; now it's home to the Griffin Theatre Company, dedicated to nurturing new Australian writers. It's also where many actors started out – Cate Blanchett and David Wenham both trod the boards here early in their careers. Rush tickets ($15) are available on the day

## Understand

### Sydney Cinema

Since Fox Studios opened in Moore Park in 1998, Sydney has starred in various blockbusters such as the *Matrix* trilogy, *Mission Impossible 2* and *X-Men Origins: Wolverine*. Sydneysider Baz Luhrmann's *Moulin Rouge, Australia* and *The Great Gatsby* were made here, as were numerous other films set everywhere from Antarctica *(Happy Feet II)* to a galaxy far, far away (the Star Wars prequels).

Yet more emblematic of the soul of Sydney cinema is the decidedly low budget **Tropfest** (www.tropfest.com), where thousands of locals shake out their blankets in The Domain to watch entries in the largest short-film festival in the world.

#### Beginnings

One of the most successful early Australian films was *The Sentimental Bloke* (1919), which included scenes filmed in Manly, the Royal Botanic Gardens and Woolloomooloo. Government intervention in the form of both state and federal subsidies reshaped the future of the country's film industry through the 1970s. Sydneysiders who benefitted from the subsequent renaissance in the industry included Oscar-nominated director Peter Weir (who made such films as *Gallipoli, Dead Poets Society, The Truman Show* and *Master and Commander*) and Oscar winners Mel Gibson and Nicole Kidman.

#### Boom & Beyond

The 1990s saw films that cemented Australia's reputation as a producer of quirky comedies about local misfits: *Strictly Ballroom* (with locations in Pyrmont and Marrickville), *Muriel's Wedding* (Parramatta, Darlinghurst and Darling Point) and *The Adventures of Priscilla, Queen of the Desert* (Erskineville). Sydney actors who got their cinematic start around this time include Hugo Weaving, David Wenham, New Zealand–born Russell Crowe, Cate Blanchett, Heath Ledger and Toni Collette.

The new millennium got off to a good start with the likes of *Lantana* and *Finding Nemo*, but since then it's fair to say that Sydney has failed to set big screens alight.

Holy Kitsch!

of certain performances. (☏9361 3817; www.griffintheatre.com.au; 10 Nimrod St; tickets $15-49; ℞King Cross)

### Gaelic Club
LIVE MUSIC

27 ⭐ Map p98, A5

Whether it's the latest darlings of the British music press or some local sonic assailants made good, concerts at the midsize Gaelic bridge the gap between the pub scene and the larger theatres. (☏9211 1687; www.thegaelic .com; 64 Devonshire St; tickets free-$50; ℞Central)

### Govinda's
CINEMA

28 ⭐ Map p98, E2

The Hare Krishna Govinda's is an all-you-can-gobble vegetarian smorgasbord, including admission to the movie room upstairs. Expect mainstream blockbusters, art-house classics, incense in the air and cushions on the floor. (☏9380 5155; www.govindas .com.au; 112 Darlinghurst Rd; dinner & movie $30, movie only $14; ☉sessions 7-9.15pm Tue-Thu, 4.30-9.45pm Fri-Sun; ℞Kings Cross)

## Shopping

### Surry Hills Markets
MARKET

29 🔒 Map p98, C5

There's a chipper community vibe at this monthly market, with mainly locals renting stalls to sell/recycle their old stuff: clothes, CDs, books and sundry junk. Bargains aplenty; if only it was more frequent! (www.shnc.org /markets; Shannon Reserve, Crown St; ☉7am-4pm 1st Sat of the month; ℞Central)

### Artery
ART

30 🔒 Map p98, E2

Step into a world of mesmerising dots and swirls at this small gallery devoted to Aboriginal art. Artery's motto is 'ethical, contemporary, affordable', and while large canvases by more established artists cost in the thousands, small, unstretched canvases start at around $35. (☏9380 8234; www.artery .com.au; 221 Darlinghurst Rd; ☉10am-6pm Mon-Fri, 11am-4pm Sat & Sun; ℞Kings Cross)

OLIVER STREWE / GETTY IMAGES ©

### Bookshop Darlinghurst BOOKS

**31** Map p98, D3

This outstanding bookshop specialises in gay and lesbian tomes, with everything from queer crime and lesbian fiction to glossy pictorials and porn. A diverting browse, to say the least. (☎9331 1103; www.thebookshop.com.au; 207 Oxford St; ☺10am-10pm; ◙Kings Cross)

### Sydney Antique Centre ANTIQUES

**32** Map p98, D6

Sydney's oldest antique centre has 50-plus dealers specialising in porcelain, silver, glass, collectables and furniture. Items range from sports memorabilia to antique grandfather clocks and art deco jewellery. Pick up a 19th-century alabaster mannequin and drag it around the cafe and bookshop. (☎9361 3244; www.sydantcent.com.au; 531 South Dowling St; ☺10am-6pm; ▯339)

### Holy Kitsch! GIFTS

**33** Map p98, C4

When you've a hole that only Day of the Dead and Mexican wrestling paraphernalia can fill, here's where you come. (www.holykitsch.com.au; 321 Crown St; ☺11am-6.30pm; ◙Central)

### Wheels & Dollbaby CLOTHING

**34** Map p98, C3

'Clothes to Snare a Millionaire' is the name of the game here, and what a wicked, wicked game it is: lace, leather and leopard print, studs, suspenders and satin. Tightly wrapped and trussed up; it won't just be the millionaires who'll be looking your way. Male rockers will have to settle for T-shirts. (☎9361 3286; www.wheelsanddollbaby.com; 259 Crown St; ☺10am-6pm Mon-Wed, Fri & Sat, to 8pm Thu, noon-5pm Sun; ◙Museum)

### Blue Spinach CLOTHING, ACCESSORIES

**35** Map p98, E2

High-end consignment clothing for penny-pinching label lovers of all genders. If you can make it beyond the shocking blue facade (shocking doesn't really do it justice), you'll find Paul Smith and Gucci at (relatively) bargain prices. (☎9331 3904; www.bluespinach.com.au; 348 Liverpool St; ☺10am-6pm Mon-Sat, 11am-4pm Sun; ◙Kings Cross)

### Grandma Takes a Trip CLOTHING, ACCESSORIES

**36** Map p98, C3

We don't know where granny's gone, but she sure left a crazy wardrobe behind. And so did grandpa. Sourced mostly in the UK and overseas, this is mint-condition vintage, plus retro swimwear and the odd bit of flouncy lingerie. (☎9356 3322; www.grandmatakesatrip.com; 263 Crown St; ☺10am-6pm Sat-Wed, to 8pm Thu; ◙Central)

## Local Life
# A Saturday in Paddington

**Getting There**

🚌 Routes 378 (Railway Sq to Bronte) and 380 (Circular Quay to Watsons Bay via Bondi) head along Oxford St. Route 389 (Circular Quay to Bondi) takes the back roads.

Paddington is an elegant neighbourhood of beautifully restored terrace houses and steep leafy streets where fashionable folks (seemingly without the need to occupy an office) drift between designer boutiques, art galleries and bookshops. Built over an ancient track used by the Cadigal people, the suburb's pulsing artery is Oxford St. The liveliest time to visit is on Saturday, when the markets are effervescing.

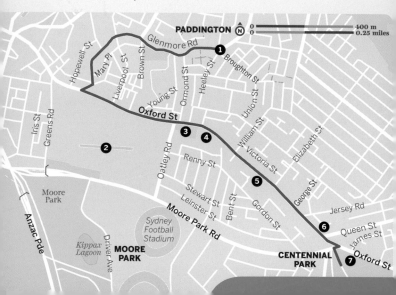

### ❶ Hang out in Five Ways

Oxford St may be the main drag, but the quirky cafes, galleries, shops and pub at the star-like junction of Five Ways make it the hip heart of Paddington. Start your sojourn with coffee in **Sonoma** (www.sonoma.com.au; 241 Glenmore Rd; mains $10-16; ⏱7am-4pm; 🚌389), a bakery-cafe specialising in sourdough bread and popular with the yummy-mummy set.

### ❷ Peer at Victoria Barracks

A manicured vision from the peak of the British Empire, these Georgian **barracks** (☎8335 5170; Oxford St; admission free; ⏱tours 10am Thu; 🚌380), built 1841–48, have been called the finest of their kind in the colonies. They're still an active army base, so unless you return for the Thursday tour you'll have to peer through the gates.

### ❸ Stroll through Paddington Reservoir Gardens

Opened to much architectural acclaim in 2008, this impressive **park** (cnr Oxford St & Oatley Rd; 🚌380) makes use of Paddington's long-abandoned 1866 water reservoir, incorporating the brick arches and surviving chamber into an interesting green space featuring a sunken garden, pond, boardwalk and lawns.

### ❹ Visit the Australian Centre for Photography

The nonprofit **ACP** (☎9332 0555; www.acp.org.au; 257 Oxford St; admission free; ⏱noon-7pm Tue-Fri, 10am-6pm Sat & Sun; 🚌380) exhibits the photographic gems of renowned Sydney and international photographers. It's particularly passionate about photomedia, video and digital-imaging works.

### ❺ Experience Paddington Markets

A cultural experience, these quirky, long-running markets turn Saturdays in Paddington into pandemonium. In the 1970s, when they started, **Paddington Markets** (☎9331 2923; www.paddingtonmarkets.com.au; 395 Oxford St; ⏱10am-4pm Sat; 🚌380) were distinctly counter-cultural. It's a tad more mainstream now, but still worth checking out for new and vintage clothing, creative crafts, jewellery, food, palm-reading and holistic treatments.

### ❻ Relax in the Wine Library

With an impressive range of wines by the glass and a stylish but casual feel, this little **bar** (18 Oxford St, Woollahra; ⏱11.30am-11.30pm Mon-Fri, 10am-11.30pm Sat, 10am-10pm Sun; 🚌380) is a sophisticated pitstop for battle-hardened shoppers. The Mediterranean-inclined menu is excellent too.

### ❼ Explore Centennial Park

Scratched out of the sand in 1888 in grand Victorian style, Sydney's biggest **park** (☎9339 6699; www.centennialparklands.com.au; Oxford St; ⏱vehicles sunrise-sunset; 🚆Bondi Junction) is a rambling 189-hectare expanse full of horse riders, joggers, cyclists and in-line skaters.

Explore

# Kings Cross & Potts Point

If Darling Harbour is Sydney dressing up nicely for tourists, the Cross is where it relaxes, scratches itself and belches. In equal parts thrilling and depressing but never boring, this is the go-to zone for late-night blinders. In gracious, tree-lined Potts Point and Elizabeth Bay, well-preserved Victorian, Edwardian and art deco houses flank picturesque streets.

GLENN VAN DER KNIJFF / GETTY IMAGES ©

# The Sights in a Day

 Start your day with breakfast at **Uliveto** (p117). Take a stroll along Darlinghurst Rd, reading the bronze social history plaques set into the footpath along the way. The El Alamein Fountain marks the beginning of **Fitzroy Gardens** (p117); stop to rummage through the weekend markets. Continue down to Elizabeth Bay and spend the rest of the morning in **Elizabeth Bay House** (p117). Wander up the stairs near 17 Billyard Ave and head to **Fratelli Paradiso** (p118) for lunch.

Continue along Challis Ave, admiring the impressive row of colonnaded mansions. At the end, there's a great view over Woolloomooloo from Embarkation Park. Turn left and stroll along leafy Victoria St. If you're planning a big night, head back to your accommodation for a pre-disco nap. Otherwise while away the afternoon in the **Gazebo Wine Garden** (p120).

Grab dinner at **Ms G's** (p118) and then hit the bars and clubs.

For a local's day in Kings Cross & Potts Point, see p114.

 **Local Life**

Wandering around Woolloomooloo (p114)

 **Best of Sydney**

**Historic Buildings**
Elizabeth Bay House (p117)

**Markets**
Fitzroy Gardens (p117)

## Getting There

🚆 **Train** Everywhere is within walking distance of Kings Cross station, although the western fringe of Woolloomooloo is closer to St James.

🚌 **Bus** Route 311 hooks through Kings Cross, Potts Point, Elizabeth Bay and Woolloomooloo on its circuitous route from Railway Sq. Buses 324 and 325 (Circular Quay–Watsons Bay) pass through Bayswater Rd in Kings Cross.

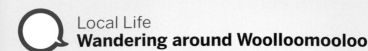

## Local Life
# Wandering around Woolloomooloo

Squeezed between The Domain and Kings Cross, Woolloomooloo (show us another word with eight Os!) is a suburb in transition. Once solidly working class, it still has some rough edges but down by the water they're hard to spot. The navy base is still here, but drunken sailors are in short supply.

❶ **Descend McElhone Stairs**

These stone stairs were built in 1870 to connect spiffy Potts Point with the Woolloomooloo slums below. The steep steps run past an apartment block: residents sip tea on their balconies and stare bemusedly at the fitness freaks punishing themselves on the 113-stair uphill climb.

❷ **Snack at Harry's Cafe de Wheels**

Sure, it's a humble pie cart, but **Harry's** (☏9347 3074;

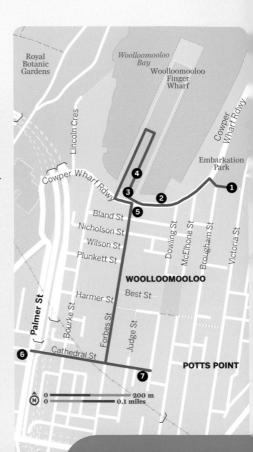

www.harryscafedewheels.com.au; Cowper Wharf Rdwy; pies $3-4; ⏱9am-1am Sun, 8.30am-3am Mon-Sat; 🚍311) is a tourist attraction nonetheless. Open since 1938 (except for a few years when founder Harry 'Tiger' Edwards was on active service), Harry's has served the good stuff to everyone from Pamela Anderson to Frank Sinatra and Colonel Sanders.

**❸ Woolloomooloo Finger Wharf**
A former wool and cargo dock, this beautiful Edwardian wharf faced oblivion for decades before a 2½-year demolition-workers' green ban on the site in the late 1980s saved it. It received a huge sprucing up in the late 1990s and has emerged as one of Sydney's most exclusive eating, drinking, sleeping and marina addresses.

**❹ Relax in the Waterbar**
After a few martinis in the heart of Woolloomooloo's Finger Wharf, time becomes meaningless and escape pointless. Lofty, romantic **Waterbar** (☎8356 2553; www.waterbaratblue.com; Woolloomooloo Finger Wharf; ⏱5-10pm Sun & Mon, to midnight Tue-Sat; 🚉Kings Cross) sucks you in to its pink-love world of candles, corners, deep lounges and ottomans as big as beds. Great for business (if you really must), but better for lurve.

**❺ Space out in Artspace**
**Artspace** (☎9356 0555; www.artspace.org .au; 43-51 Cowper Wharf Rdwy; admission free; ⏱11am-5pm Tue-Sun; 🚉Kings Cross)

is spacey: its eternal quest is to fill the void with vigorous, engaging Australian and international contemporary art. Things here are decidedly avant-garde – expect lots of conceptual pieces, AV installations and new-media masterpieces. It's an admirable attempt to liven things up in Sydney's art scene, experimenting with sometimes-disturbing concepts.

**❻ Top up at Toby's Estate**
Coffee is undoubtedly the main event at this cool little charcoal-coloured roaster, but **Toby's Estate** (☎9358 1196; www.tobysestate.com.au; 129 Cathedral St; meals $9-15; ⏱breakfast & lunch; 🚉St James) is also a great place for a quick baguette, a lamb salad or a wedge of cake. And the caffeine? Strong, perfectly brewed and usually fair trade.

**❼ Settle in at the Old Fitzroy**
Islington meets Melbourne in the back streets of Woolloomooloo: this totally unpretentious theatre **pub** (☎9356 3848; www.oldfitzroy.com.au; 129 Dowling St; ⏱11am-midnight Mon-Sat, 3-10pm Sun; 🚉Kings Cross) is also a decent old-fashioned boozer in its own right. There are airy street-side tables and a grungy upstairs area with a pool table and scruffy lounges.

A | B | C | D

Woolloomooloo Bay

1

Woolloomooloo
Finger
Wharf

**POTTS POINT**

Wylde St

Cowper Wharf Rdwy

0 ——————— 200 m
0 ——————— 0.1 miles

N

**For reviews see**

◉ Sights p117
✕ Eating p117
🍷 Drinking p120

St Neot Ave

Mcdonald St

Mcdonald La

Embarkation
Park

Challis Ave

9 ✕

Elizabeth
Bay

2

5 ✕
6 ✕

Cowper Wharf Rdwy

Billyard Ave

Bland St

Nicholson St

Rockwall La

Rockwall Cres

7 ✕ Elizabeth
Bay
House

Arthur
McElhone
Reserve

Beare
Park

Billyard Ave

**WOOLLOOMOOLOO**

10 ✕

Manning St

Crick Ave

◉ 1

Onslow Ave

3

Best St

Stephen St

Hughes St

Crick Ave

Greenknowe Ave

John Armstrong
Reserve

Ithaca Rd

Forbes St

Judge St

Dowling St

McElhone St

Brougham St

Victoria St

Orwell St

Earl St

Macleay St

Llankelly Pl

4 ✕

**ELIZABETH
BAY**

Elizabeth Bay Rd

Lawrence
Hargrave
Park

Roslyn Gdns

Evans Rd

Waratah Rd

Cathedral St

4

8 ✕

17 🍷  19 🍷
18 🍷

Earl Pl

15 🍷

◉ 2
Fitzroy
Gardens

14 ✕🍷

11 ✕

Rushcutters
Bay Park

**RUSHCUTTERS
BAY**

Kings
Cross

Brougham La

13 🍷

12 🍷

Kellett St

16 🍷

Pennys La

Goderich La

Kings Cross Rd

**KINGS
CROSS**

Ward Ave

Roslyn St

Bayswater Rd

3 ✕

Waratah St

William St

5

# Sights

### Elizabeth Bay House
HISTORIC BUILDING

1  Map p116, D3

Completed in 1839 for Colonial Secretary Alexander Macleay, this elegant, neoclassical mansion by architect John Verge was one of the finest houses in the colony (and still is). Its grounds – a sort of botanical garden for Macleay, who collected plants from around the world – once extended from the harbour all the way up the hill to Kings Cross. (☎9356 3022; www.hht.net.au; 7 Onslow Ave; adult/child/family $8/4/17; ☺9.30am-4pm Fri-Sun; ☒Kings Cross)

### Fitzroy Gardens
PARK

2  Map p116, C4

It's testimony to the 'cleaning up' of the Cross that this once-dodgy park is now a reasonably safe place to hang out (probably helped by the austere police station in the corner). The dandelion-esque El Alamein Fountain (1961) sends waves of chlorinated spray across the open space. An organic food market sets up here on Saturday mornings. (cnr Macleay St & Darlinghurst Rd; ☒Kings Cross)

# Eating

### Uliveto
CAFE $

3  Map p116, C5

Beautiful all-day eggy breakfasts, scrummy muffins, fresh juices and top-notch coffee are the staples of this chilled-out cafe, set in a tree-lined plaza. The people-watching is not bad either. Check your foam; this place is known for its 'latte art'. (☎9357 7331; www.ulivetocafe.com.au; 33 Bayswater Rd; mains $10 19; ☺breakfast & lunch; ☒Kings Cross)

### Room 10
CAFE $

4  Map p116, C4

If you're wearing a flat cap, sprouting a beard and obsessed by coffee,

---

### Understand
#### Where Exactly is Kings Cross?

Where exactly is Kings Cross? Although technically it's just the intersection of William and Victoria Sts (where the streets named after two kings cross; ok, so one's a queen, but let's not split hairs), in reality it's more of a mindset than an exact geographical place. What most people call Kings Cross falls within the suburb of Potts Point; businesses tend to use a Potts Point address if they want to sound classy and Kings Cross if they want to emphasise their party cred. Either way, you'll know Kings Cross when you see it.

chances are you'll recognise this tiny room as your spiritual home in the Cross. The food's limited to sandwiches, salads and such – tasty and uncomplicated. (10 Llankelly Pl; mains $8-12; ⊗breakfast & lunch; 🚇Kings Cross)

## Otto Ristorante ITALIAN $$$

5  Map p116, A2

Forget the glamorous waterfront location and the A-list crowd – Otto will be remembered for single-handedly dragging Sydney's Italian cooking into the new century with dishes such as *strozzapreti con gamberi* (artisan pasta with fresh Yamba prawns, tomato, chilli and black olives). Bookings essential. (✆9368 7488; www.ottoristorante.com.au; Woolloomooloo Finger Wharf; mains $38-44; ⊗lunch & dinner; 🚇Kings Cross)

## Aki's INDIAN $$

6  Map p116, A2

The first cab off the rank as you walk onto Woolloomooloo's wharf is Aki's. And you need walk no further: this is beautifully presented, intuitively constructed high-Indian cuisine, supplemented by a six-page wine list showcasing local and international drops by the glass or bottle. The Keralan chilli beef is a simmering sensation. (✆9332 4600; www.akisindian.com.au; 1/6 Cowper Wharf Rdwy; mains $21-36; ⊗lunch Sun-Fri, dinner daily; 🛜🖊; 🚇Kings Cross)

## Zinc CAFE $$

7  Map p116, C3

Zinc was built on breakfasts, and the kitchen continues to create too many hard decisions for 7am. It doesn't get much easier choosing between the tasty sandwiches and salads offered at lunchtime or the range of bistro dinners. The good-looking staff are full of smiles. (✆9358 6777; www.cafezinc.com.au; 77 Macleay St; breakfast $8.50-14, lunch $8.50-19, dinner $25-27; ⊗breakfast & lunch daily, dinner Tue-Sat; 🖊; 🚇Kings Cross)

## Ms G's ASIAN $$

8  Map p116, B4

Offering a cheeky, irreverent take on Asian cooking (hence the name – geddit?), Ms G's is nothing if not an experience. It can be loud, frantic and painfully hip, but the adventurous combinations of Vietnamese, Thai, Korean, Chinese, Taiwanese and European flavours have certainly got Sydney talking. (✆9240 3000; www.merivalecom; 155 Victoria St; mains $16-29; ⊗lunch Fri & Sun, dinner daily; 🚇Kings Cross)

## Fratelli Paradiso ITALIAN $$

9  Map p116, C2

This underlit trattoria has them queuing at the door (especially on weekends). The intimate room showcases seasonal Italian dishes cooked with Mediterranean zing: lots of busy black-clad waiters, lots of Italian chatter, lots of oversized sunglasses – somehow Rome doesn't seem so far

away... No bookings. (📞9357 1744; www
.fratelliparadiso.com; 12-16 Challis Ave; mains
$22-31; ⏰7am-11pm Mon-Sat, 7am-6pm Sun;
🚉Kings Cross)

## Cafe Sopra ITALIAN $$

10  Map p116, C3

Attached to the mighty impressive
Fratelli Fresh provedore, Sopra serves
no-fuss, perfectly prepared Italian food
in a bustling atmosphere. The huge
menu changes seasonally, but some
favourites (eg the fabulous *rigatoni
alla bolognese*) are constants. (www
.fratellifresh.com.au; 81 Macleay St; mains
$18-28; ⏰lunch & dinner daily; 🚉Kings Cross)

## Piccolo Bar CAFE $

11  Map p116, C4

A surviving slice of the old bohemian
Cross, this tiny cafe hasn't changed
much in nearly 60 years. The walls are
covered in movie star memorabilia,
the battered jukebox plays Marianne
Faithfull and Paolo Conti, and Vittorio
Bianchi still serves up strong coffee,
omelettes and abrasive charm as he's
done for more than 30 years. (www
.piccolobar.com.au; 6 Roslyn St; mains $9-15;
⏰6am-2am; 📶; 🚉Kings Cross)

## Guzman y Gomez MEXICAN $

12  Map p116, B5

A spicy alternative for fast-food
aficionados, this zippy diner uses the
freshest local produce to whip up
authentic Mexican tacos, burritos and
quesadillas. Everything's marinated
and grilled daily. Look out for other
branches around Sydney. (www.guzmany
gomez.com; cnr Bayswater Rd & Pennys La;
mains $7.50-11; ⏰11am-10pm Sun-Thu, 11am-
4am Fri & Sat; 🚉Kings Cross)

---

### Understand
### **Rugby League**

There's plenty to yell about if you arrive during the winter footy season.
'Footy' can mean a number of things – Australian Rules football (Aussie
Rules), rugby union and soccer – but in Sydney's it's usually rugby league.

Rugby league is king in NSW, and Sydney is considered one of the world
capitals for the code. The pinnacle of the game is widely held to be the annual State of Origin where NSW battles Queensland. This best-of-three
series even overshadows test matches, such as the annual Anzac Test
between Australia's Kangaroos and New Zealand's Kiwis.

The National Rugby League comp runs from March to October, climax-
ing in the sell-out grand final at ANZ Stadium. You can catch games every
weekend during the season, played at the home grounds of Sydney's various tribes. The easiest ground to access is the 45,500-seat Sydney Football
Stadium, home of the Sydney Roosters.

# Drinking

## Kings Cross Hotel
PUB, LIVE MUSIC

**13** Map p116, B5

With five floors above ground and one below, this grand old pub is a hive of boozy entertainment that positively swarms on weekends. Best of all is FBi Social, an alternative radio station–led takeover of the second floor, bringing with it an edgy roster of live music. The roof bar has DJs on weekends and awesome city views. (www.kingscross hotel.com.au; 244-248 William St; ⊘noon-3am Sun-Thu, noon-6am Fri & Sat; ᯤKings Cross)

## Gazebo Wine Garden
WINE BAR

**14** Map p116, C4

A hip wine bar in skanky old Fitzroy Gardens? Who would have believed it 10 years ago? This place has groovy decor (wrought-iron gates, bespoke benches, eclectic couches) and a hi-tech vino storage system that shoots gas into open bottles (meaning that 55 sometimes obscure wines are available by the glass to join the 300 by the bottle). (✆9357 5333; www.gazebowinegarden .com.au; 2 Elizabeth Bay Rd; ⊘3pm-midnight Mon-Thu, noon-midnight Fri-Sun; ᯤKings Cross)

Jimmy Liks

## Sugarmill
BAR

15  Map p116, B4

For a bloated, late-night, Kings Cross bar, Sugarmill is actually pretty cool. Columns and high pressed-tin ceilings hint at its banking past, while the band posters plastered everywhere do their best to dispel any lingering capitalist vibes. Cheapskates feast on cheap steaks daily, while on Friday nights a hip dude with a guitar duels with TV sports. (www.sugarmill.com.au; 33 Darlinghurst Rd; ⏰10am-5am; 🚊Kings Cross)

## World Bar
BAR, CLUB

16  Map p116, B5

World Bar (a reformed bordello) is an unpretentious grungy club with three floors to lure the backpackers in and cheap drinks to loosen things up. DJs play indie, hip hop, power pop and house nightly. Propaganda (indie classics, new and used) on Thursday provides a sure-fire head-start to your weekend. Live bands on Friday. (☎9357 7700; www.theworldbar.com; 24 Bayswater Rd; admission free-$15; ⏰2pm-late; 🚊Kings Cross)

## Soho
BAR, CLUB

17  Map p116, B4

Inside this art deco hotel is a dark, sexy establishment where the smooth leather lounges have felt the weight of Keanu Reeves', Nicole Kidman's and Ewan McGregor's celebrity booties. It's rumoured to be where Kylie met Michael Hutchence. Downstairs, the club pumps out electro, house and dub from Thursday to Saturday. (www.sohobar.com.au; 171 Victoria St; ⏰10am-midnight Mon-Wed, 10am-4am Thu, 10am-6am Fri, 9am-6am Sat, 9am-4am Sun; 🚊Kings Cross)

## Kit & Kaboodle
CLUB

The club above Sugarmill (see 15  Map p116, B4) comes into its own on a Sunday night, when hospitality workers take advantage of the cheap drinks to kick-start their belated weekend. (www.kitkaboodle.com.au; 33 Darlinghurst Rd; admission free-$10; ⏰8pm-late Thu-Sun; 🚊Kings Cross)

## Bootleg
BAR

18  Map p116, B4

If you're looking for a quieter, sophisticated alternative to the Darlinghurst Rd melee (or just a chance to catch your breath), slink into a booth at this bar-cum-Italian eatery and order a wine from the list. The decor's a mix of industrial-chic and Chicago lounge bar, but it works. (www.bootlegbar.com.au; 175 Victoria St; ⏰4-11pm Sun, Tue & Wed, 4pm-1am Thu-Sat; 🚊Kings Cross)

## Jimmy Liks
COCKTAIL BAR

19  Map p116, B4

Understated, slim and subtle, Jimmy's is very cool, with benches almost as long as the Southeast Asian–influenced cocktail list (try a Mekong Mary with chilli vodka and *nam jim*). (☎8354 1400; www.jimmyliks.com; 186-188 Victoria St; ⏰5pm-midnight; 🚊Kings Cross)

Explore

# Bondi to Coogee

Improbably good-looking arcs of sand framed by jagged cliffs, the Eastern Beaches are a big part of the Sydney experience. Most famous of all is the broad sweep of Bondi Beach, where the distracting scenery and constant procession of beautiful bods never fail to take your mind off whatever it was you were just thinking about...

## The Sights in a Day

☀ Grab your swimming gear and head to the beach. Catch the bus to **Bondi** (p124) and spend some time strolling about and soaking it all in. If the weather's right, stop for a swim. Once you're done, take the clifftop path to **Tamarama Beach** (p128) and on to **Bronte Beach** (p128). Take a slight detour up to Bronte's excellent **Three Blue Ducks** (p130) for lunch.

☀ Continue on the coastal path through **Waverley Cemetery** (p128), **Clovelly Beach** (p128) and on to **Coogee Beach** (p128). Board a bus back to wherever you're staying and freshen up for the night ahead.

☾ Have a beer on the terrace of the **North Bondi RSL** (p131) as the sun goes down and then pop downstairs to **North Bondi Italian Food** (p130) for dinner with a view. Finish up with a cocktail at **Icebergs Bar** (p131) or gear up for a raucous evening at **Beach Road Hotel** (p131).

 **Top Sights**

Bondi Beach (p124)

♥ **Best of Sydney**

**Eating**
Icebergs Dining Room (p129)

Three Blue Ducks (p130)

North Bondi Italian Food (p130)

**Beaches**
Bondi Beach (p124)

Bronte Beach (p128)

Clovelly Beach (p128)

Tamarama Beach (p128)

**Markets**
Bondi Markets (p132)

## Getting There

🚆 **Train** The Eastern Suburbs line heads to Bondi Junction, which is 2.5km from Bondi Beach.

🚌 **Bus** For Bondi catch bus 333 (express), 380, 381, 382 or 389. For Bronte take bus 378. For Clovelly take bus 339 or 360. For Coogee take bus 373 via Oxford St, bus 372 via Surry Hills, or bus 313, 314 or 353 from Bondi Junction.

# Top Sights
## Bondi Beach

Definitively Sydney, Bondi is one of the world's great beaches: ocean and land collide, the Pacific arrives in great foaming swells and all people are equal, as democratic as sand. It is the closest ocean beach to the city centre (8km away), has consistently good (though crowded) waves, and is great for a rough-and-tumble swim. If the sea's angry or you have small children in tow, try the saltwater sea baths at either end of the beach.

Map p126, D2

Campbell Pde

380

Bondi Beach

# Don't Miss

## Bondi Pavilion

Built in the Mediterranean Georgian Revival style in 1929, **Bondi Pavilion** (📞8362 3400; www.waverley .nsw.gov.au; Queen Elizabeth Dr; admission free; ⏰9.30am-5.30pm; 🚌380) is more cultural centre than changing shed, although it does have changing rooms, showers and lockers. **Bondi Openair Cinema** (📞Moshtix 1300 438 849; www.bondiopenair.com.au; tickets $22) takes place on the lawn in the summer months. 'The Pav' is also home to a gelateria and a bar-restaurant.

## Surf Lessons

Bondi is a great beach for learning to surf. **Let's Go Surfing** (📞9365 1800; www.letsgosurfing.com.au; 128 Ramsgate Ave), down the far northern end of the beach, caters to practically everyone, with classes for grommets (ages seven to 16; 1½ hours $49) and adults (two hours $99). If you just want to hire gear to hit the waves, you can do that too.

## Dry Land Activities

Prefer wheels to fins? There's a skate ramp at the beach's southern end. And if posing in your budgie smugglers (speedos) isn't having enough impact, there's an outdoor workout area near the North Bondi Surf Club. Coincidentally (or perhaps not), this is the part of the beach where the gay guys hang out.

## Bondi Icebergs

With supreme views of Bondi Beach, **Bondi Icebergs** (📞9130 4804; www.icebergs.com.au; 1 Notts Ave; adult/child $5.50/3.50; ⏰6.30am-6.30pm Fri-Wed; 🚌380) is a fair dinkum Sydney institution. Only hardened winter-swimming fanatics can become fully fledged members, but anyone can pay for a casual entry.

---

## ☑ Top Tips

▶ The two surf clubs (Bondi and North Bondi) patrol the beach between sets of red and yellow flags, positioned to avoid the worst rips and holes. Thousands of unfortunates have to be rescued from the surf each year (enough to make a TV series about it), so don't become a statistic – swim between the flags.

▶ At the beach's northern end there's a grassy spot with coin-operated barbecues.

▶ Surfers carve up sandbar breaks at either end of the beach.

## ✗ Take a Break

Soak up the views from the Crabbe Hole (p130) cafe.

Booze is banned on the beach, so head up to the North Bondi RSL (p131) for a cooling beer on the terrace.

Aboriginal
Rock
Engravings **6**

Bondi
Golf Club

Military Rd

Bay St

Ben Buckler
Point

**7**

Wallis Pde

Hastings Pde

Brighton Blvd

Ramsgate Ave

**11**

Walora Ave

Bondi
Bay

**10**

Bondi
Pavilion

Bondi
Beach

Blair St

Warners Ave

Gould St

Campbell Pde

**20**

**12**

**8**

Marks
Park

Beach Rd

Curlewis St

**13**

Hunter
Park

Wilga St

Fletcher St

Mackenzies
Bay

Glenayr Ave

**19**

**22**

Gaerloch Ave

Silva St

Dudley St

Tamarama
Bay

**15**

**21**

LAMROCK AVE

BONDI
BEACH

Glen St

Gaerloch
Reserve

Tamarama
Beach

**3**

Tamarama
Bay

Roscoe St

Hall St

O'Brien St

Cox Ave

Francis St

Denham St

**14**

TAMARAMA

Tamarama
Park

Cross St

Hewlett St

Bronte
Beach

**1**

Wellington St

Old South Head Rd

Edward St

Avoca St

Alfred St

Belgrave St

Read St

Hewlett St

Bronte
Park

Bayview St

Bronte Rd

Gardyne St

Bennelong Cres

Birriga Rd

Bellevue
Park

Martins Ave

Wellington St

Watson St

BONDI

**23**

King St

Stephen St

Ewell St

Birrell St

Palmerston Ave

Victoria Rd

Bellevue Rd

Cooper
Park

BELLEVUE HILL

Ocean St N

Penkivil St

Bondi Rd

Angelesea St

Park Pde

Waverley
Park

Paul St

BONDI
JUNCTION

Wiley St

Henrietta St

WAVERLEY

Gibson St

Murray St

Gipps St

BRONTE

Paul St

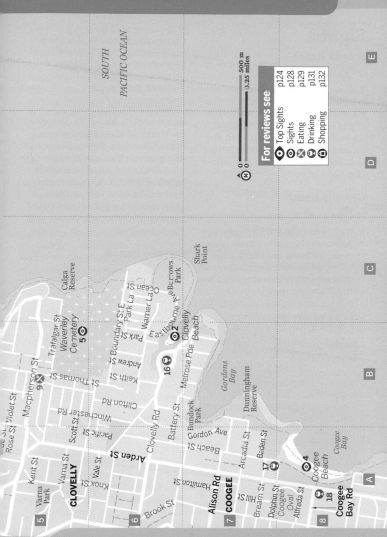

SOUTH
PACIFIC OCEAN

**For reviews see**

| | | |
|---|---|---|
| ● | Top Sights | p124 |
| ⊙ | Sights | p128 |
| ✕ | Eating | p129 |
| ● | Drinking | p131 |
| ● | Shopping | p132 |

bow-tied waiters deliver fresh seafood and steaks cooked with élan. The bar is also a stunner. (☎9365 9000; www.idrb.com; 1 Notts Ave; mains $36-54; ⊙lunch & dinner Tue-Sun; ☐380)

### Three Blue Ducks
CAFE $$

9  Map p126, B5

These ducks are a 500m waddle from the water but that doesn't stop queues forming outside the graffiti-covered walls for weekend breakfasts. The adventurous owners have a strong commitment to using local, organic and fair-trade food whenever possible. (www.threeblueducks.com; 143 Macpherson St; breakfast $12-19, lunch $18-26, dinner shared plates $17; ⊙breakfast & lunch Tue-Sun, dinner Thu-Sat; ☐378)

### Harry's Espresso Bar
CAFE $

10  Map p126, D1

Harry's game is coffee and he's winning down this end of the beach. For breakfast, try a 'smashed croissant' – a croissant that's been squashed and then slathered with ricotta, blueberries, almonds and mint. Everything comes with a side order of graffiti art. (136 Wairoa Ave; mains $7-14; ⊙breakfast & lunch; ☐380)

### North Bondi Italian Food
ITALIAN $$

11  Map p126, E2

As noisy as it is fashionable, this terrific trattoria in the North Bondi Returned and Services League (RSL) building has a casual vibe, simple but *molto delizioso* food and a democratic no-booking policy. Come early to snaffle a table overlooking the beach. (www.idrb.com; 118-120 Ramsgate Ave; mains $18-34; ⊙lunch Fri-Sun, dinner daily; ☐380)

### Pompei's
ITALIAN $$

12  Map p126, D2

The pizza here is among the best in Sydney, but it's the northern Italian dishes whipped up by explosive expat George Pompei that are really special. Try the handmade ravioli stuffed with spinach, ricotta and nutmeg, and leave some space for a scoop of white peach gelato. (☎9365 1233; www.pompeis.com.au; 126-130 Roscoe St; mains $19-33; ⊙lunch Fri-Sun, dinner Tue-Sun; ☐380)

### Crabbe Hole
CAFE $

Tucked within the Bondi Icebergs complex (see 8  Map p126, D3) – there's no need to pay admission if you're only eating) – this crab-sized nook is the kind of place locals would prefer wasn't in this book. Toasted sandwiches, muesli and banana bread star on the small but perfectly formed menu; coffees are automatic double shots unless you wimp out. The views are blissful. (Lower Level, 1 Notts Ave; mains $10-12; ⊙7am-5pm; ☐380)

### Earth Food Store
CAFE, DELI $

13  Map p126, C2

An organic cafe, deli and naturopath under one roof, this place serves up a healthy range of salads, quiches, sushi, panini and tennis-ball-sized falafel, plus takeaway nuts, herbs, spices, teas, fruit and veg. (☎9365 5098; www.earth foodstore.com.au; 81 Gould St; mains $4-16; ◷6.30am-5.30pm; ☒; ☒380)

# Drinking

## North Bondi RSL BAR

This bar in the RSL building (see 11  Map p126, E2) ain't fancy, but with views no one can afford and drinks that everyone can, who cares? Bring ID, as nonmembers need to prove that they live at least 5km away. There are live bands most Saturdays, trivia on Tuesdays and cheap steaks on Wednesdays. (☎9130 3152; www.northbondirsl.com.au; 120 Ramsgate Ave; ◷noon-midnight Mon-Thu, 10am-midnight Fri-Sun; ☒380, 389)

## Corner House BAR

14 ☻ Map p126, C3

Three spaces – the Kitchen (wine bar), Dining Room (restaurant) and Living Room (bar) – make this a happy house, especially once you hit the cocktails. (www.thecornerhouse.com.au; 281 Bondi Rd; ◷5pm-midnight Mon-Fri, 3pm-midnight Sat, 3-10pm Sun; ☒380)

## Icebergs Bar BAR

Most folk come here to eat next door at the Icebergs Dining Room (see 8  Map p126, D3), but the ooh-la-la Icebergs Bar is a brilliant place for a drink. The hanging chairs, colourful sofas and ritzy cocktails are fab, but the view looking north across Bondi Beach is the absolute killer. Dress sexy and make sure your bank account is up to the strain. (☎9365 9000; www.idrb.com; 1 Notts Ave; ◷noon-midnight Tue-Sat, to 10pm Sun; ☒380)

## Beach Road Hotel PUB, DJ

15 ☻ Map p126, C1

Weekends at this big, boxy pub are a boisterous multilevel alcoholiday, with Bondi types (bronzed, buff and brooding) and woozy out-of-towners playing pool, drinking beer and digging live bands and DJs. (☎9130 7247; www.beach roadbondi.com.au; 71 Beach Rd; ◷10am-1am Mon-Sat, 10am-10pm Sun; ☒389)

TRAVELSCAPE IMAGES / ALAMY ©

Icebergs Bar

### Clovelly Hotel
PUB, DJ

16  Map p126, B6

A recently renovated megalith on the hill above Clovelly Beach, this pub has a shady terrace and water views – perfect for postbeach Sunday afternoon beverages and the sleepy sounds of acoustic twangers. Singer-songwriters strum their stuff on Thursdays and DJs crank it up on weekends. (☏9665 1214; www.clovellyhotel.com.au; 381 Clovelly Rd; ⏰10am-midnight Mon-Fri, 8am-midnight Sat, 8am-10pm Sun; ☒339)

### Aquarium
BAR, DJ

17 🍸 Map p126, A7

On the top floor of the historic Beach Palace Hotel (1887), a massive booze barn at the northern end of Coogee Beach, Aquarium is a good place to be on a Sunday afternoon. The views from the terrace are awesome; DJs and live acoustic acts provide the theme tunes. (☏9664 2900; www.beach palacehotel.com.au; 169 Dolphin St; ⏰4pm-midnight Fri, noon-midnight Sat & Sun; ☒372-374)

### Coogee Bay Hotel
PUB, CLUB

18 🍺 Map p126, A8

This rambling, rowdy complex still packs in the backpackers for live music, open-mic nights, comedy and big-screen sports in the beaut beer garden, sports bar and Selina's nightclub. Sit on a stool in the window overlooking the beach and sip on a cold one. (☏9665 0000; www.coogeebay hotel.com.au; cnr Coogee Bay Rd & Arden St;

⏰9am-3am Mon-Thu, to 5am Fri & Sat, to midnight Sun; ☒372-374)

# Shopping

### Surfection
CLOTHING, ACCESSORIES

19 🔒 Map p126, C2

Selling boardies, bikinis, sunnies, shoes, watches, tees...even luggage – Bondi's coolest surf store has everything the stylish surfer's heart might desire (except for spray-in hair bleacher; you'll still need to take your paper bag to a discreet chemist for that). Old boards hang from the ceiling, while new boards fill up the racks (JS, Al Merrick, Takayama). (www.surfection.com; 31 Hall St; ☒380)

### Bondi Markets
MARKETS

20 🔒 Map p126, D1

The kids are at the beach on Sunday while their school fills up with Bondi characters rummaging through tie-dyed, secondhand clothes, books, beads, earrings, aromatherapy oils, candles, old records and more. There's a farmers market on Saturdays. (☏9315 8988; www.bondimarkets.com.au; Bondi Beach Public School, Campbell Pde; ⏰9am-1pm Sat, 10am-4pm Sun; ☒380)

### Gertrude & Alice
BOOKS

21 🔒 Map p126, C2

This shambolic secondhand bookshop and cafe is so un-Bondi: there's not a model or surfer in sight. Locals, students and academics hang out

Coogee Bay Hotel

reading, drinking coffee and acting like Americans in Paris. Join them for some lentil stew and theological discourse around communal tables. (📞9130 5155; www.gertrudeandalice.com.au; 46 Hall St; ⏰7.30am-10pm; 🚌380)

## Rip Curl
CLOTHING, ACCESSORIES

**22** 🔒 Map p126, C2

The quintessential Aussie surf shop, Rip Curl began down south in Victoria, but drops in perfectly overlooking the Bondi shore breaks. Beyond huge posters of burly surfer dudes and beach babes, you'll find bikinis, watches, thongs, boardshorts, wetsuits, sunglasses, hats, T-shirts and (surprise!) surfboards. (📞9130 2660; www.ripcurl.com; 82 Campbell Pde; ⏰9am-6pm; 🚌380)

## Kemenys
WINE

**23** 🔒 Map p126, B2

A short walk up (and then a wobble down) the hill from Bondi Beach, Kemenys occupies a large soft spot in the hearts, minds and livers of all Bondi locals. Proffering the best local and imported wines, ales and spirits to the surf set since 1960, it's staunchly resisted being taken over by the big chains. Respect. (📞13 88 81; www.kemenys.com.au; 137-147 Bondi Rd; ⏰8am-9pm; 🚌380)

## Local Life
# A Day in Watsons Bay

The narrow peninsula ending in South Head is one of Sydney's most sublime spots. The view of the harbour from the Bondi approach, as Old South Head Rd leaves the sheer ocean cliffs to descend to Watsons Bay, is breathtaking. Watsons Bay was once a small fishing village, as evidenced by the tiny heritage cottages that pepper the suburb's narrow streets.

### Getting There

🚢 Regular ferries run between Circular Quay and Watsons Bay.

🚌 Routes to Watsons Bay include the 325 via Vaucluse and bus the 380 via Bondi.

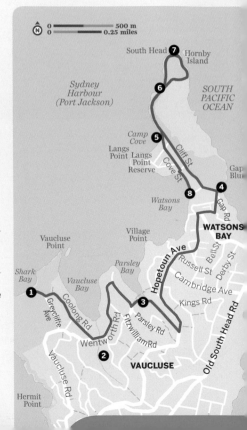

## ❶ Nielsen Park

Visit this shady remnant of the 206-hectare Vaucluse estate on a weekday when it's not too busy. The park encloses **Shark Beach** – a great spot for a swim, despite the ominous name – and **Greycliffe House**, a beautiful 1851 Gothic sandstone pile (not open to visitors).

## ❷ Vaucluse House

**Vaucluse House** (www.hht.net.au; Wentworth Rd; adult/child/family $8/4/17; ⏱9.30am-4pm Fri-Sun; ▢325) is an imposing, turreted specimen of Gothic Australiana set among 10 hectares of lush gardens. The house was started in 1805 and tinkered with into the 1860s. Decorated with European period pieces, the house offers visitors a rare glimpse into early (albeit privileged) colonial life in Sydney.

## ❸ Parsley Bay

A hidden gem, this little bay has a calm swimming beach, a lawn dotted with sculptures for picnics and play, and a cute suspension bridge. Keep an eye out for water dragons as you walk down through the bush.

## ❹ The Gap

On the ocean side of Watsons Bay, The Gap is a dramatic cliff-top lookout where proposals and suicides happen with similar frequency.

## ❺ Camp Cove

Immediately north of Watsons Bay, this swimming beach is popular with both families and topless sunbathers. When Governor Phillip realised Botany Bay didn't cut it as a site for a settlement, he sailed north into Sydney Harbour, dropped anchor and sunk his boots into Camp Cove's gorgeous golden sand on 21 January 1788.

## ❻ Lady Bay

Also known as Lady Jane, this diminutive gay nudist beach sits at the bottom of a cliff, on top of which is a Royal Australian Navy facility. To get here, follow the cliff-top walking track from Camp Cove.

## ❼ South Head

The **South Head Heritage Trail** passes old battlements and a path heading down to Lady Bay, before continuing on to the candy-striped Hornby Lighthouse and the sandstone Lightkeepers' Cottages (1858) on South Head itself. The harbour views and crashing surf on the ocean side make this a very dramatic and beautiful spot indeed.

## ❽ Watsons Bay Hotel

One of the great pleasures in life is languishing in the rowdy beer garden of the **Watsons Bay Hotel** (www.watsonsbayhotel.com.au; 1 Military Rd, Watsons Bay; ⏱10am-11pm; ▢Watsons Bay) with a jug of sangria after a day at the beach. Stay to watch the sun go down over the city and grab some seafood if you're hungry.

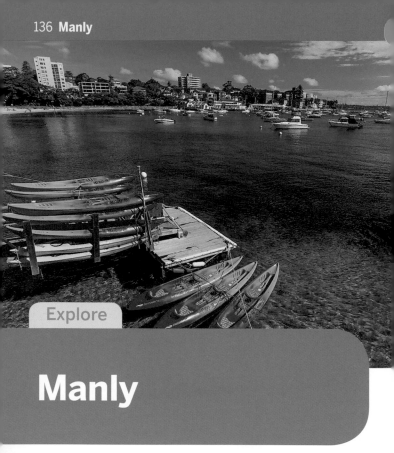

Explore

# Manly

Laid-back Manly clings to a narrow isthmus between ocean and harbour beaches abutting North Head, Sydney Harbour's northern gatepost. With its shaggy surfers, dusty labourers and relaxed locals, it makes for a refreshing change from the stuffier harbour suburbs nearby. The surf's good and as the gateway to the Northern Beaches, it makes a popular base for the board-riding brigade.

## The Sights in a Day

☀ Jump on the ferry at Circular Quay for the leisurely and extremely beautiful journey to Manly. Before it gets too hot, hire a bike from **Manly Bike Tours** (p141), grab a map at the visitor centre on the wharf opposite, and explore **North Head** (p139), dropping into **Q Station** (p139), the historic former quarantine station, on the way back. Return the bikes, cool off with a dip at **Manly Cove** (p140) and head to **Belgrave Cartel** (p141) for lunch.

☀ It'll take less than an hour to breeze around **Manly Art Gallery & Museum** (p140). If you're not planning on visiting Darling Harbour's Sydney Aquarium, **Oceanworld** (p140) is a trimmed down alternative – plus you can swim with sharks here. Head along the **Corso** (p140) and spend the rest of the day body-surfing and lazing around **Manly Beach** (p139).

☾ Shuffle into a seat with a view at **Hugos Manly** (p142) on Manly Wharf and order pizza. Finish up with a drink on the water's edge at **Manly Wharf Hotel** (p143) or sample the range at the **Bavarian Bier Café** (p143).

 **Best of Sydney**

**Drinking**
Bavarian Bier Café (p143)

**Beaches**
Manly Beach (p139)
Store Beach (p139)

**For Free**
Manly Art Gallery & Museum (p140)

## Getting There

🚢 **Ferry** Frequent ferry services head directly from Circular Quay, making this by far the best (and most scenic) means to get to Manly. Regular Sydney ferries take 30 minutes while fast ferries take 18 minutes.

🚌 **Bus** Prepay express bus E70 takes 37 minutes to reach Manly Wharf from the city, while regular bus 171 takes about an hour.

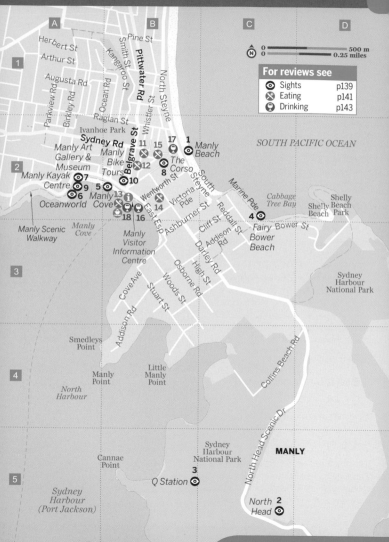

A · B · C · D

Herbert St
Arthur St
Augusta Rd
Parkview Rd
Birkley Rd
Raglan St

Pine St
Smith St
Kangaroo Rd
Ocean Rd
Pittwater Rd
North Steyne
Whistler St

Ivanhoe Park
**Sydney Rd**
Manly Art
Gallery &
Museum
Manly
Bike
Tours
**Belgrave St**

Manly Kayak
Centre
Oceanworld
Manly Cove

Manly Scenic
Walkway

Manly
Cove

Manly
Visitor
Information
Centre

Cove Ave
Stuart St
Addison Rd
Woods St
Osborne Rd
High St
Darley Rd
Addison Rd
Cliff St
Reddall St
Ashburner St
Victoria Pde
South Steyne
Wentworth St
East Esp

11 · 15 · 17 · 1 · Manly Beach
The Corso
12 · 8
10 · 13 · 14 · 16 · 18
7 · 9 · 5 · 6

*SOUTH PACIFIC OCEAN*

Marine Pde
Fairy Bower St
4 · Fairy Bower Beach
Cabbage Tree Bay
Shelly Beach
Shelly Beach Park

Smedleys Point

Manly Point

Little Manly Point

*North Harbour*

Collins Beach Rd
North Head Scenic Dr

Sydney Harbour National Park

**MANLY**

Cannae Point

Sydney Harbour National Park
3 · Q Station

*Sydney Harbour (Port Jackson)*

North Head · 2

**N** 0 — 500 m
0 — 0.25 miles

**For reviews see**
◉ Sights        p139
✕ Eating       p141
☻ Drinking    p143

# Sights

## Manly Beach                    BEACH

**1** ◉ Map p138, B2

Manly Beach stretches for nearly two golden kilometres, lined by Norfolk Island pines and scrappy midrise apartment blocks. The southern end of the beach, nearest the Corso, is known as South Steyne, with North Steyne in the centre and Queenscliff at the northern end; each has its own surf lifesaving club. (🏖Manly)

## North Head                    OUTDOORS

**2** ◉ Map p138, C5

About 3km south of Manly, chunky North Head offers dramatic cliffs, lookouts and sweeping views of the ocean, the harbour and the city; hire a bike and go exploring. A 9km, four-hour walking loop is outlined in the Manly Scenic Walkway brochure, available from the visitor centre. Magical **Store Beach** can only be reached by kayak or boat. (North Head Scenic Dr; 🚌135)

## Q Station                    HISTORIC BUILDING

**3** ◉ Map p138, B5

The eerie but elegant Manly Quarantine Station was used to isolate newly arrived epidemic-disease carriers between 1828 and 1972. It was then used until 1984 to house illegal immigrants. These days the 'Q Station' has been reborn as a tourist destination, with a museum and a whole swag of tour op-

tions, including a 2½-hour Ghost Tour ($44 to $52). (📞9466 1500; www.qstation .com.au; 1 North Head Scenic Dr; admission free; 🕐museum 10am-2pm Mon-Thu, 10am-2pm & 5-8pm Fri, 10am-8pm Sat, 10am-4pm Sun; 🚌135)

## Fairy Bower Beach                    BEACH

**4** ◉ Map p138, C2

Indulge your mermaid fantasies (the more seemly ones at least) in this pretty triangular ocean pool set into the rocky shoreline. The life-size sea nymphs of Helen Leete's bronze sculpture *Oceanides* (1997) stands on the edge, washed by the surf. Fairy Bower is best reached by the promenade

OLIVER STREWE / CORBIS ©

Cafe at Fairy Bower Beach

heading around Manly Beach's south
headland. (Bower St; 🚌135)

## Manly Cove
BEACH

**5**  Map p138, B2

Split in two by Manly Wharf, this sheltered enclave has shark nets and calm
water, making it a popular choice for
families with toddlers. Despite the
busy location, the clear waters have
plenty of appeal. (🚢Manly)

## Oceanworld
AQUARIUM

**6**  Map p138, A2

This ain't the place to come if you're
on your way to Manly Beach for
a surf. Inside this daggy-looking
1980s building are underwater glass
tubes through which you become
alarmingly intimate with 3m sharks.
Reckon they're not hungry? **Shark
Dive Xtreme** (📞8251 7878; introductory/
certified dives $270/195) takes you into
their world... Crocodiles and large
turtles also put in an appearance.

(📞8251 7877; www.oceanworld.com.au; West
Esplanade; adult/child/family $20/10/48;
🕙10am-5.30pm, last admission 4.45pm;
🚢Manly)

## Manly Art Gallery & Museum
GALLERY, MUSEUM

**7**  Map p138, A2

A short stroll from Manly Wharf is
this passionately managed community
gallery, maintaining a local focus with
exhibits of surfcraft, swimwear and
beachy bits and pieces. There's also a
ceramics gallery, and lots of old Manly
photos to peer at. (📞9976 1420; www
.manly.nsw.gov.au; West Esplanade; admission
free; 🕙10am-5pm Tue-Sun; 🚢Manly)

## The Corso
STREET

**8**  Map p138, B2

The quickest route from the Manly
ferry terminal to Manly's ocean beach
is along the Corso, a part-pedestrian
mall lined with surf shops, pubs and
sushi bars. Kids splash around in

---

### Understand
### Surf Lifesaving

Surf lifesaving originated in Sydney, although red-and-yellow-capped volun-
teer lifesavers have since assumed iconic status across Australia. Despite
the macho image, many lifesavers are women, and a contingent of gay and
lesbian lifesavers march in the Sydney Mardi Gras parade.

At summer surf carnivals all along the coast you can see these dedicated
athletes wedge their speedos up their butt cracks and launch their surf
boats (butt cheeks grip the seats better than speedos, apparently). Ask a
local surf lifesaving club for dates, or contact **Surf Life Saving Australia**
(📞9471 8000; www.surflifesaving.com.au) for info.

the fountains and spaced-out surfies shuffle back to the ferry after a hard day carving up the swell. The mood is suburban and relaxed. (Manly)

## Manly Kayak Centre
KAYAKING

 9 Map p138, A2

As long as you can swim, you can hire a kayak or paddle board from this stand near Oceanworld (with a second stand near Manly Wharf Hotel). You'll be provided with a life jacket, paddling instruction and tips on secluded beaches to visit. Three-hour kayak tours cost $89. (1300 529 257; www.manlykayakcentre.com.au; West Esplanade; 1/2/8hr from $20/35/70; 9am-6pm Dec-Feb, reduced hours Mar-Nov; Manly)

## Manly Bike Tours
CYCLING

 10 Map p138, B2

Come here to hire a bike to tackle North Head or take a two-hour tour around Manly ($89; bookings essential), departing at 10.30am daily. (8005 7368; www.manlybiketours.com.au; 54 West Promenade; hire per hr/day from $14/28; 9am-6pm; Manly)

# Eating

## Barefoot Coffee Traders
CAFE $

 11 Map p138, B2

Run by surfer lads from a bathroom-sized shop, Barefoot heralds a new wave of Manly cool. Food is limited but the Belgian chocolate waffles go magi-

cally well with macchiato. They have a second cafe opposite the wharf which works symbiotically with its neighbour Adriano Zumbo; grab some sublime patisserie and devour it along with a coffee. (0412 328 810; www.barefoot coffee.com.au; 18a Whistler St; items $3-6; breakfast & lunch; Manly)

## Belgrave Cartel
CAFE $

 12 Map p138, B2

Little Cartel may be grungy but it's nowhere near as sinister as it sounds; the only drug being peddled here is pure, unadulterated caffeine. 'Mismatched everything' seems to be the design brief and the food is restricted to the likes of panini and toasted sandwiches (called 'jaffles' in these parts) but it's certainly tasty and served with a smile. (6 Belgrave St; mains $5-13; ⏰ breakfast & lunch daily, dinner Thu; 🛳 Manly)

## Hugos Manly

ITALIAN **$$**

**13** 🍴 Map p138, B2

Staking out an altogether more glamorous location than its Kings Cross parent, Hugos Manly serves the same acclaimed pizzas but tops them with harbour views. (☎ 8116 8555; www .hugos.com.au; Manly Wharf; pizzas $20-28, mains $32-38; ⏰ lunch & dinner; 🛳 Manly)

## Chat Thai

THAI **$**

Set inside Manly Wharf with Hugos Manly (see 13 🍴 Map p138, B2), this branch of the Thaitown favourite misses out on the harbour views from its location inside the wharf but delivers on flavour. (☎ 9976 2939; www. chatthai.com.au; Manly Wharf; mains $10-19; ⏰ lunch & dinner; 🛳 Manly)

## Pure Wholefoods

VEGETARIAN **$**

**14** 🍴 Map p138, B2

This wholefood minimart has a great little street cafe serving organic vegetarian goodies, including flavour-

Dining on Manly Wharf

## Local Life
**Manly-Warringah Sea Eagles**

The local rugby league team are neighbourhood heroes, having won the premiership twice in the last decade. Home games are played further north at Brookvale, but Manly's pubs are lively places to watch matches. The local pub scene revolves around the Corso and Manly Wharf.

some salads, nori rolls, cakes, cookies, wraps, burgers and smoothies. Vegan, sugar-free, gluten-free and dairy-free purists are also catered for. (☏8966 9377; www.purewholefoods.com.au; 10 Darley Rd; mains $10-15; ☺breakfast & lunch; ✈; ☻Manly)

### BenBry Burgers                BURGERS $

**15**  Map p138, B2

A popular takeaway assembling juicy burgers for beach bums and backpackers. (www.benbrybugers.com.au; 5 Sydney Rd; burgers $8-14; ☺lunch & dinner; ☻Manly)

# Drinking

## Manly Wharf Hotel              PUB

**16**  Map p138, B2

Harking back to 1950s design (feature walls in bamboo and stone), the

Manly Wharf Hotel is perfect for sunny afternoon beers. Tuck away a few schooners after a hard day in the surf, then pour yourself onto the ferry. Sports games draw a crowd and DJs liven up Sunday afternoons. Great pub food, too, with specials throughout the week. (☏9977 1266; www.manlywharfhotel.com.au; Manly Wharf; ☺11.30am-midnight Mon-Sat, 11am-10pm Sun; ☻Manly)

### Hotel Steyne                  PUB

**17**  Map p138, B2

Boasting numerous bars over two levels, this landmark pub accommodates everyone from sporty bogans to clubby kids to families. The courtyard isn't flash (people still smoke here!), but the rooftop bar more than makes up for it with wicked views over the beach. Live bands and DJs entertain. (☏9977 4977; www.steynehotel.com.au; 75 The Corso; ☺9am-3am Mon-Sat, 9am-midnight Sun; ☻Manly)

### Bavarian Bier Café            BEER HALL

**18** Map p138, B2

The Bavarian offers 10 brews on tap and 10 more imported beers by the bottle. Soak it all up with some bratwurst, sauerkraut and a schnitzel right by the water's edge. (www.bavarianbiercafe.com; Manly Wharf; ☺11am-midnight Mon-Fri, 9am-midnight Sat & Sun; ☻Manly)

# The Best of
# **Sydney**

### Sydney's Best Walks

### Sydney's Best...

Cafe dining, Bondi
OLIVER STREWE / GETTY IMAGES ©

## Best Walks
# The City's Green Corridor

### 🏃 The Walk

There's no better introduction to Sydney's top sights than this stroll through the corridor of parkland that runs through the heart of Sydney, ending in the organised chaos of Circular Quay. The route can be marched in an hour, or stretched out to the best part of a day, with extended stops along the way.

**Start** Anzac Memorial; 🚌 Museum

**Finish** Circular Quay; 🚌 Circular Quay

**Length** 5km; two hours

### 🍴 Take a Break

There are cafes and restaurants in the Art Gallery and Royal Botanic Gardens, or you could hold on until Circular Quay for a ritzy meal at **Aria** (p36) or a cheaper bite at **Sailors Thai Canteen** (p36).

Royal Botanic Gardens (p26)

### ❶ Anzac Memorial

The dignified 1934 **Anzac Memorial** (p52) commemorates the soldiers of the Australian and New Zealand Army Corps (Anzac) who served in WWI. The interior dome is studded with 120,000 golden stars – one for each man and woman from NSW who served. The centrepiece, Rayner Hoff's sculpture *Sacrifice*, is particularly poignant.

### ❷ Hyde Park

Leave the memorial by the northern door and head straight through the centre of **Hyde Park** (p52), past the **Pool of Remembrance**. Hyde Park is split in two by Park St; cross over and continue through the avenue of trees to the **Archibald Memorial Fountain**.

### ❸ The Domain

Veer right at the fountain, cross towards the ornate **Lands Department Building** and enter **The Domain** (p54). On Sunday afternoons zealots express their earnest opinions at the by turns entertaining and enraging **Speakers' Corner** on the lawn in front of the **Art Gallery of NSW** (p46).

### ❹ Mrs Macquaries Point

The Domain ends in spectacular fashion at **Mrs Macquaries Point** (p27), where a vista of the harbour, Fort Denison, Opera House, Harbour Bridge and city skyline suddenly appears. Clouds of sulphur-crested cockatoos disturb the peace with their raucous caws during the day; at night it's a romantic spot for an after-dinner stroll.

### ❺ Royal Botanic Gardens

Follow the swoop of Farm Cove into the beautiful surrounds of the **Royal Botanic Gardens** (p26). Keep an eye out for **Government House** as you pass beneath it.

### ❻ Sydney Opera House

As you exit through Queen Elizabeth II Gate the heaven-sent sails of the **Sydney Opera House** (p24) are directly in front of you.

Clamber up to their base and circumnavigate Bennelong Point to enjoy it from every angle.

### ❼ Sydney Writers Walk

A series of metal discs cast into the Circular Quay promenade hold ruminations from prominent Australian writers (and the odd literary visitor).

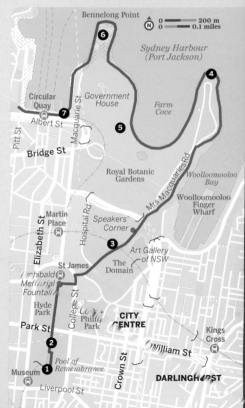

# Best Walks
# Bondi to Coogee

## 🏃 The Walk

Arguably Sydney's most famous, most popular and best walk, this coastal path shouldn't be missed. Both ends are well connected to bus routes, as are most points in between should you feel too hot and bothered to continue – although a cooling dip at any of the beaches en route should cure that (pack your swimmers). There's little shade on this track, so make sure you dive into a tub of sunscreen before setting out.

**Start** Bondi Beach; 🚌 380

**Finish** Coogee Beach; 🚌 372, 373

**Length** 6km; three hours

## 🍴 Take a Break

The best lunch option is Bronte's **Three Blue Ducks** (p130). To get there, cut through the reserve immediately before Waverley Cemetery and head up Macpherson St.

### ❶ Bondi Beach

Starting at **Bondi Beach** (p124), take the stairs up the south end to Notts Ave, passing above the glistening Bondi Icebergs pool complex. Step onto the clifftop trail at the end of Notts Ave. Walking south, the blustery sandstone cliffs and grinding Pacific Ocean couldn't be more spectacular (watch for dolphins, whales and surfers).

### ❷ Tamarama Beach

Small but perfectly formed **Tamarama Beach** (p128) has a deep reach of sand, totally disproportionate to its width.

### ❸ Bronte Beach

Descend from the cliff tops onto **Bronte Beach** (p128) and take a dip or hit a beachy cafe for a coffee, a chunky lunch or a quick snack. Cross the sand and pick up the path on the other side.

ANDREW WATSON / GETTY IMAGES ©

Clifftop trail from Bondi to Coogee

### ④ Waverley Cemetery

Some famous Australians are among the subterranean denizens of the amazing cliff-edge **Waverley Cemetery** (p128). On a clear day this is a prime vantage point for whale-watchers.

### ⑤ Clovelly Beach

Duck into the sunbaked **Clovelly Bowling Club** for a beer or a game of bowls, then breeze past the cockatoos and canoodling lovers in **Burrows Park** to sheltered **Clovelly Beach** (p128), a fave with families.

### ⑥ Gordons Bay

Follow the footpath up through the car park, along Cliffbrook Pde, then down the steps to the upturned dinghies lining **Gordons Bay**, one of Sydney's best shore-dive spots.

### ⑦ Dolphin Point

This grassy tract at Coogee Beach's northern end has superb ocean views and the Giles Baths ocean pool. A sobering shrine commemorates the 2002 Bali bombings. Coogee was hit hard by the tragedy, with 20 of the 89 Australians killed coming from hereabouts. Six members of the Coogee Dolphins rugby league team died in the blast.

### ⑧ Coogee Beach

The trail then lands you smack-bang on glorious **Coogee Beach** (p128). Swagger up to the **Aquarium** (p132) bar at the Beach Palace Hotel and toast your efforts with a cold lager.

# Best Walks
# Manly Scenic Walkway

## 🏃 The Walk

This epic walk traces the coast west from Manly past million-dollar harbour-view properties and then through a rugged 2.5km section of Sydney Harbour National Park that remains much as it was when the First Fleet sailed in. Make sure you carry plenty of water, slop on some sunscreen, slap on a hat and wear sturdy shoes.

**Start** Manly Cove; 🚢 Manly

**Finish** Spit Bridge; 🚌 176-180 (to city), 140-144 (to Manly)

**Length** 9km; four hours

## ✕ Take a Break

There aren't any eateries en route, so fortify yourself in Manly beforehand or stock up for a picnic at **Pure Wholefoods** (p142) and **Adriano Zumbo Patisserie** (cnr East Esplanade & Wentworth St, Manly; ⏱7am-7pm Mon-Fri, 8am-5.30pm Sat & Sun).

IGNACIO PALACIOS / GETTY IMAGES ©

Spit Bridge

## ❶ Manly Cove

Pick up a walk brochure (which includes a detailed map) from the **visitor information centre** (p176) by Manly Wharf. Walk along **Manly Cove** (p140) and pick up the path near **Oceanworld** (p140).

## ❷ Fairlight Beach

After 700m you'll reach **Fairlight Beach**, where you can scan the view through the heads. Yachts tug at their moorings as you trace the North Harbour inlet for the next 2km.

## ❸ Forty Baskets Beach

**Forty Baskets Beach** sits at the point where the well-heeled streets of Balgowlah Heights end and bushclad Sydney Harbour National Park commences. The picnic area is cut off at high tide.

## ❹ Reef Beach

Kookaburras cackle as you enter the national park and approach **Reef Beach**. Despite what you might have heard, this little cove is neither nude nor full of dudes; the Manly Council put pay to that in 1993. Now it's often deserted.

## ➎ Dobroyd Head

The track becomes steep, sandy and rocky further into the park – keep an eye out for wildflowers, spiders in bottlebrush trees and fat goannas sunning themselves. The views from Dobroyd Head are unforgettable. Check out the deserted 1930s sea shacks at the base of Crater Cove cliff.

## ➏ Grotto Point

Look for **Aboriginal rock carvings** on an unsigned ledge left of the track before the turnoff to **Grotto Point Lighthouse**. Rugged and beautiful, **Washaway Beach** is a secluded little spot on the point's eastern edge.

## ➐ Clontarf Beach

Becalmed **Castle Rock Beach** is at the western end of the national park. From here the path winds around the rear of houses to

**Clontarf Beach**, a low-lapping elbow of sand facing the Spit Bridge that's popular with families, with grassy picnic areas.

## ➑ Spit Bridge

Sandy Bay follows and then Fisher Bay before you reach Spit Bridge, a bascule bridge that connects Manly to Mosman and opens periodically to let boats through to Middle Harbour.

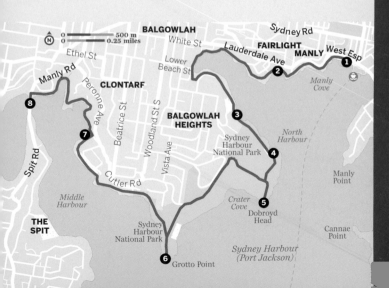

# Best
# **Beaches**

Whether you join the procession of the bronzed and the beautiful at Bondi, or surreptitiously slink into a deserted nook hidden within Sydney Harbour National Park, the beach is an essential part of the Sydney experience. Even in winter, watching the rollers break while you're strolling along the sand is exhilarating.

TONY BURNS / GETTY IMAGES ©

## Best Harbour Beaches

**Shark Beach** The pick of the harbour beaches, hidden within leafy Nielsen Park. (p135)

**Camp Cove** Family-friendly, with golden sand and gentle swells. (p135)

**Store Beach** You'll need to paddle your way to this isolated North Head beach. (p139)

**Lady Bay** Discreetly tucked under South Head, this is the best of the nude beaches. (p135)

## Best Ocean Beaches

**Bondi Beach** Australia's most famous beach, for good reason. (p124)

**Clovelly Beach** Despite the concrete, this is a magical swimming and snorkelling spot. (p128)

**Bronte Beach** Perfect for bucket-and-spade family days and picnic lunches. (p128)

**Manly Beach** Learn to surf or simply laze upon the 2km of golden sand. (p139)

**Tamarama Beach** Treacherous waves pound this pretty scoop of sand. (p128)

 **Top Tips**

▶ Always swim between the red and yellow flags on lifesaver-patrolled beaches. Not only are these areas patrolled, they're positioned away from dangerous rips and holes.

▶ Due to pollution from stormwater drains, avoid swimming in the ocean for one day and in the harbour for three days after heavy rains.

# Best
# Historic Buildings

CHEE-ONN LEONG / SHUTTERSTOCK.COM ©

## Best Homes

**Vaucluse House** William Wentworth's Vaucluse mansion is a rare surviving colonial harbourside estate. (p135)

**Elizabeth Bay House** Another harbourside home, built in a gracious Georgian style in the heart of Lizzie Bay. (p117)

**Susannah Place** Giving the people who lived in slum houses their rightful place in history. (p32)

## Best Religious Buildings

**St Mary's Cathedral** Beamed in from Gothic Europe, the grand Catholic cathedral is awash with colour when the sun hits the stained glass. (p52)

**Great Synagogue** A mismatch of architectural styles, maybe, but a beautiful one. (p54)

**St James' Church** Francis Greenway's elegant, understated church is perhaps his crowning achievement. (p54)

**St Andrew's Cathedral** Based on York Minster,

the city's Anglican cathedral stakes its place in Sydney society next to the Town Hall. (p54)

**Sze Yup Temple** A surprising find on the edge of Glebe, this small Chinese temple is perpetually wreathed in incense. (p83)

## Best Administrative Buildings

**Town Hall** The Victorians may have seemed buttoned up, but not when it came to their buildings, as the exuberant Town Hall attests. (p54)

**Hyde Park Barracks** Convict architect Francis Greenway's beautiful prison, housing a fascinating museum. (p48)

**Victoria Barracks** Still used by the military, these Georgian army barracks can be visited on free guided tours. (p111)

## Best Commercial Buildings

**Queen Victoria Building** The most unrestrained

and ornate survivor of the Victorian era. (p62)

**Martin Place** A stretch of grand bank buildings and the High Victorian former General Post Office, the most iconic building of its time. (p49)

# Best
# Eating

PIXNXT / GETTY IMAGES ©

Sydney's cuisine rivals that of any world city. Melbourne makes a big deal of its Mediterranean melting pot, but Sydney truly celebrates Australia's place on the Pacific Rim, marrying the freshest local ingredients with the flavours of Asia, the Americas and, of course, its colonial past. For more information on Sydney's food culture, see p73.

## Where to Eat

Sydney's top restaurants are properly pricey, but eating out needn't be expensive. There are plenty of ethnic eateries where you can grab a cheap, zingy pizza or a bowl of noodles. Cafes are a good bet for a solid, sometimes adventurous and usually reasonably priced, meal.

## Advance Australian Fare

Australia is blessed with first-rate produce from farms and fisheries across the nation. The tropical north provides pineapples, mangoes and even winter strawberries, while cooler southern climes lend themselves to fine wines and cheeses. These come together in a fresh, flavoursome, multicultural collision on dining tables across Sydney.

## Wine & BYO

Most licensed restaurants have a good wine list and there's almost always at least a handful of wines sold by the glass. Sydney is blessed with enlightened licensing laws that allow you to BYO (bring your own) wine and sometimes beer to restaurants with a BYO licence. You'll usually be charged a corkage fee (even if your bottle's got a screw cap) at either a per-person or per-bottle rate, but it's generally cheaper than choosing off the wine list.

## ☑ Top Tips

▶ Tipping isn't compulsory in Australia, but if the service is passable most folks tip 10% (particularly at better restaurants). If anything gets on your goat, you don't have to tip at all. Tipping isn't expected at cafes, but there's often a jar where customers can sling loose change.

## Best Modern Australian

**Quay** Inventive fine dining with the best views in Sydney. (p34)

**Marque** Boundary-pushing dishes in a formal setting. (p103)

Tetsuya's (p55) signature dish – confit of ocean trout with fennel

## Best Italian

**Icebergs Dining Room** Seafood and steaks by the seashore. (p129)

**North Bondi Italian Food** Terrific trattoria above an iconic stretch of coast. (p130)

## Best Thai

**Chat Thai** Reasonably priced, loaded with flavour and constantly buzzing. (p56)

**Longrain** Delicious modern Thai concoctions and piquant cocktails. (p103)

## Best Chinese

**Spice Temple** An atmospheric underground den dealing in intense flavours. (p56)

**Bar H** Modern Chinese in a hip setting. (p103)

## Best Japanese Fusion

**Sepia** Japanese-influenced fine dining at the top of its game. (p55)

**Tetsuya's** Book months ahead for this groundbreaking restaurant's Japanese-French degustation. (p55)

## Best for Meat

**Porteño** Delicious slow-cooked meat and bucketloads of atmosphere. (p102)

**Rockpool Bar & Grill** Succulent steaks and dry-aged Wagyu burgers, served amid elegant surrounds. (p56)

## Best Cafes

**Three Blue Ducks** Serves the sort of creative cafe fare that Sydney excels in. (p130)

**Single Origin Roasters** Serious caffeine fiends serving tasty bites too. (p104)

## Best Bakeries

**Adriano Zumbo** The macaron man spreads joy in multiple Sydney locations. (p72)

**Central Baking Depot** Provides tasty sustenance for office workers and tourists alike. (p56)

# Best
# Green Spaces

OLIVER STREWE / GETTY IMAGES ©

## Best Gardens

**Royal Botanic Gardens**
Well-tended lawns,
interesting botanical collections and ever-present
harbour views make this
Sydney's most beautiful
park. (p26)

**Chinese Garden of
Friendship** A tradi-
tional arrangement of
streams, ponds and
paths to soothe the city's
stresses. (p69)

## Best Formal Parks

**Hyde Park** A shady
avenue of trees, lit with
fairy lights at night,
makes this an inviting
place for a stroll. (p52)

**Victoria Park** At the
foot of the university, its
formal paths are popu-
lar with more than just
students. (p79)

## Best Open Expanses

**The Domain** The exten-
sive lawns are used for
large-scale public gather-
ings. (p54)

**Centennial Park** Formal
bits, wild bits and a whir
of joggers, cyclists and
horseriders circling the
central avenues. (p111)

## Best with Kids

**Tumbalong Park** An
urban park with an
engaging adventure
playground. (p71)

**Nielsen Park** A tucked-
away, leafy harbourside
park with a blissful shark-
netted beach. (p135)

## Best Views

**Mrs Macquaries Point**
Jutting out into the
harbour, offering the best
views of the city skyline.
(p27)

**Observatory Hill** Trudge
up from The Rocks to
this grassy knoll and
gaze over Walsh Bay.
(p32)

# Best
# With Kids

With boundless natural attractions, a climate favouring outdoor activities and an inbuilt inclination towards being laid-back, Sydney is a top spot to bring the kids. In summer there are plenty of beaches to keep everyone happy, and when it rains, there are many indoor institutions geared to the junior tourist.

WILLIAM ROBINSON / ALAMY ©

### Family & Children's Tickets

Most sights, entertainment venues and transport providers offer a discount of up to 50% off the full adult rate for children, although the upper age limit can vary widely (anything from 12 to 18 years of age). Many places also let under-fives or under-threes in for free. Family tickets are common at big attractions, generally covering two adults and two children.

### Beaches

The calm waters of Sydney's harbour beaches are great for kids. If you're particularly paranoid about sharks, head to the netted areas at Shark Beach and Manly Cove. Most of Sydney's surf beaches have free saltwater pools, meaning that dad can paddle about with the toddlers while mum goes body-surfing.

### Best Attractions for Kids

**Powerhouse Museum**
Hands-on experiments, trains, big chunks of machinery and an interactive Wiggles exhibition. (p82)

**Art Gallery of NSW** The Gallery Kids program includes free shows,

tailored discovery trails and self-guided iPod trails. (p40)

**Sydney Opera House**
Offers Kids in the House performances, including Baby Proms. (p24)

**Madame Tussauds**
Introduce your 12-year-old to Rihanna and Lady Gaga. (p71)

☑ **Top Tips**

▶ Scan kiddie shops for copies of *Sydney's Child*, a free magazine listing activities and businesses catering to anklebiters, or check the online family-events calendar at www.webchild .com.au.

▶ For an extra cost, car hire companies will supply and fit child safety seats (compulsory for children under seven).

**Sydney Aquarium** Fill in a few hours finding Nemo, sea dragons, disco-lit jellyfish, dugongs, and gargantuan rays and sharks. (p66)

# Best
# Bars & Pubs

In a city where rum was once the currency, it's little wonder that drinking plays a big part in the Sydney social scene – whether it's knocking back some tinnies at the beach, schmoozing after work, or warming up for a night on the town. Sydney offers plenty of choice in drinking establishments, from the flashy to the trashy.

BLAINE HARRINGTON III / CORBIS ©

### The Sydney Scene

Sydneysiders are generally gregarious and welcoming of visitors, and the easiest place to meet them is at the pub. Most inner-city suburbs have retained their historic corner pubs – an appealing facet of British life the colonists were loathe to leave behind. The addition of beer gardens has been an obvious improvement, as has the banning of smoking from all substantially enclosed licensed premises.

The cheapest places to drink in are the Returned and Services League (RSL) clubs. In a tourist-friendly irony, locals are barred unless they're members, but visitors who live more than 5km away are welcome (you'll need to bring proof).

### What to Wear

Sydney can be flashy, but it's also very casual. Men will nearly always get away with tidy jeans, T-shirts and trainers. Thongs (flip-flops, jandals), singlets (vests) and shorts are usually fine in pubs in the daytime, but incur security's ire after dark. Women can generally wear whatever they like, and many take this as an excuse to wear as little as possible.

☑ **Top Tips**

▶ Traditional Sydney pubs serve middies (285mL) and schooners (425mL), while pints (570mL) are the domain of Anglo-Celtic theme pubs. Australian pubs abandoned pints long ago because beer would go warm in the summer heat before you'd finished your glass.

Opera Bar (p36)

## Best Bars

**Stitch** A modern-day speakeasy hidden beneath the city's streets. (p58)

**Pocket** Alternative music, hip decor, comfy couches and table service. (p104)

**Baxter Inn** Whiskies by the dozen in a back-alley hideaway. (p58)

## Best Pubs

**Bank Hotel** Snazzily renovated pub catering to multiple Newtown subcultures. (p86)

**Hero of Waterloo** Historic pub with live music and its own dungeon. (p36)

**Courthouse Hotel** Backstreet pub with a beer garden and a wonderfully relaxed vibe. (p87)

## Best for Beer

**Lord Nelson Brewery Hotel** Arguably Sydney's oldest pub but inarguably an excellent microbrewery. (p36)

**Bavarian Bier Café** Imported beer served by the water in Manly. (p143)

## Best Wine Bars

**Wine Library** Paddington cutie with excellent food as well. (p111)

**Bambini Wine Room** Dark-wood panels and free snacks in the city centre. (p58)

## Best Cocktails

**Hinky Dinks** Happy Days are here again in this 1950s-themed cocktail bar. (p105)

**Victoria Room** Faded colonial glamour and kick-ass cocktails. (p106)

## Best Views

**Orbit** Revolve around the 47th floor of the Australia Square tower. (p59)

**Blu Bar on 36** Head up to the top of the Shangri-La for a bird's-eye view over the bridge. (p37)

## Best Outdoors

**Beresford Hotel** Join the beautiful people in Sydney's swishest beer garden. (p105)

**Opera Bar** Opera House, Harbour Bridge, Circular Quay – all present and visible. (p36)

# Best
# Gay & Lesbian

Gays and lesbians have migrated to Oz's Emerald City from all over Australia, New Zealand and the world, adding to a community that is visible, vibrant and an integral part of the city's social fabric. Locals will assure you that things aren't as exciting as they once were, but Sydney is still indisputably one of the world's great queer cities.

RICHARD KENDALL / GETTY IMAGES ©

## Social Acceptance

These days few Sydneysiders bat an eyelid at same-sex couples holding hands on the street, but the battle for acceptance has been long and protracted. Sydney is now relatively safe but it still pays to keep your wits about you, particularly at night.

## Party Time

**Mardi Gras** (www.mardigras.org.au) is the city's main gay pride festival. See p102 for more information. **Harbour City Bears** (www.harbourcitybears.com.au) runs Bear Pride Week in late August, while **Leather Pride Week** (www.sydneyleatherpride.org) is a moveable feast but usually held in winter.

Other regular parties include **Toy Box** (www.toyboxparty.com.au) at Luna Park, Sydney's most popular daytime party, and **Fag Tag** (www.fagtag.com.au), organised takeovers of straight bars.

## Best Gay Venues

**Oxford Hotel** A straight-up gay pub. (p105)

**Imperial Hotel** The home of Priscilla. (p88)

## Best Lesbian Nights

**Bank Hotel** Always popular with the Sapphic set, but especially during Lady L, a Wednesday night fixture. (p86)

☑ **Top Tips**

▸ NSW's gays and lesbians enjoy legal protection from discrimination and vilification, and an equal age of consent.

▸ Free gay and lesbian rags include the *Star Observer* (www.starobserver.com.au), *SX* (www.gaynewsnetwork.com.au) and *LOTL* (www.lotl.com).

# Best
# Performing Arts

Take Sydney at face value and it's tempting to un-fairly stereotype its good citizens as a tad shallow, with a tendency towards narcissism. But take a closer look: the arts scene is thriving, sophisticat-ed and progressive – it's not a complete accident that Sydney's definitive icon is an opera house!

PHILLIP HAYSON / GETTY IMAGES ©

### ▥ Top Tips

▶ For performance listings, check out Friday's Metro sec-tion of the *Sydney Morning Herald* (www.smh.com.au).

▶ Also check events websites www .whatsonsydney .com and http:// whatson.cityofsyd ney.nsw.gov.au.

**eatre**

atre is the most stimulating genre to explore
g your visit. Sydney doesn't have a dedicated
district, but theatre lovers don't miss out.
offers a calendar of productions from mu-
xperimental theatre at inner city venues.

all population, Australia has produced
ld's most famous opera singers,
Nellie Melba and Joan Sutherland.
may be the adored symbol of
ng such a cost-heavy art form
New works are staged, but it's
ut bums on seats.

stereotype as sun-
here's still a passionate
ere. Without having
ires of European
pired classical
t excuse to check
bourside sails.

r awesome
m tradi-
eatre.

# Best
# **For Free**

In Sydney, many of the very best things in life really are for free – especially in summer, when lazing around in the sun is one of the city's priceless pleasures.

YEO CHOON HWA

## Beaches

This ain't the Mediterranean. There are no tightly arranged lines of deckchairs awaiting your paying pleasure at Sydney beaches. Lazing on the beach is part of the Australian birthright and one that's freely available to anyone who cares to roll ou~ their towel. Many of the beaches have oce~ carved out of the rocks on their headl~ most all of those are free as well. ~ to bring sunblock, ask the surf~ are they'll give you some. ~ patrolling the beach. ~

## Best Free C~

**Art Gall~**
admi~
fr~
an~

**Muse~**
**porary**
exhibition~
but most r~
(p32)

**White Rabbit** ~
collection of cont~
porary Chinese art,~
generously displayed~
free. (p82)

## Opera

Despite its sm~
some of the wo~
including Dames~
The Opera House~
is a difficult prospect~
Sydney, but support~
the big opera hits that~

## Classical Music

Sydneysiders live with the~
soaked sports fanatics, but t~
audience for classical music ~
the extensive, highbrow repert~
cities, Sydney offers plenty of ins~
performances – offering the perfe~
out the interior of those famous ha~

## Dance

Australian dancers have a reputation f~
physical displays. Performances range fr~
tional ballet with tutus to edgy physical th~

Bangarra Dance Theatre (p38)

## Best Venues

**Sydney Opera House**
Don't miss the chance to see the House in action. (p24)

**State Theatre** We don't care what's on, visiting this beautiful place is a joy. (p60)

**City Recital Hall** The city's premier classical music venue. (p60)

**Metro Theatre** The best place to watch touring bands. (p60)

## Best Theatre Companies

**Sydney Theatre Company** The biggest name in local theatre. (p37)

**Belvoir St Theatre** Consistently excellent productions in an intimate setting. (p106)

**Griffin Theatre Company** Based at SBW Stables Theatre; nurtures new Australian writers. (p106)

## Best Dance Companies

**Sydney Dance Company** Australia's top contemporary dance troupe. (p38)

**Bangarra Dance Theatre** The nation's top Aboriginal performing artists. (p38)

**Australian Ballet** Regularly brings tutus and bulging tights to the Sydney Opera House. (p38)

**Performance Space** Edgy works staged within the cavernous surrounds of Carriageworks. (p90)

# Best **Shopping**

Brash, hedonistic Sydney has elevated shopping to a universal panacea. Feeling good? Let's go shopping. Feeling bad? Let's go shopping. Credit-card bills getting you down? Let's go shopping... Many locals treat shopping as a recreational activity rather than a necessity, evidenced by the teeming, cash-flapping masses in Pitt St Mall every weekend.

LONELY PLANET / GETTY IMAGES ©

### What to Buy

Sydney has a thriving fashion scene, and a summer dress or a pair of speedos won't take up much luggage space. Ask at the counters of CD stores or bookshops about what's hot from local bands and authors, or grab a Sydney-set DVD.

Hunter Valley wine makes a great gift.

For international travellers wanting something quintessentially Australian to take home, head to The Rocks and dig up some opals, an Akubra hat, a Driza-Bone coat or some Blundstone boots. Aboriginal art has soared to global popularity during recent decades.

## ☑ **Top Tips**

▶ By law, all sales taxes are included in the advertised price.

▶ Apart from the 10% goods and services tax (GST) the only other sales duties payable are on naughty things such as alcohol and tobacco, which are best bought at the duty-free shops at the airport.

## Best Shopping Centres

**Strand Arcade**  Fashion retail at its finest. (p62)

**Queen Victoria Building** Regal surroundings add a sense of gravitas to any splurge. (p62)

**Westfield Sydney** Bafflingly large complex incorporating top restaurants and two prestigious department stores. (p62)

## Best Bookshops

**Better Read than Dead** An interesting and eclectic range, making for great browsing. (p90)

**Gleebooks** A serious booklover's nirvana, with a healthy roster of launches and author talks. (p91)

# Best
# **Markets**

Sydney markets make for an interesting excursion. Even if you don't buy anything, the food, the buskers and the people-watching are usually worth the trip. Some markets are very touristy, but others have a distinct local vibe. They run the gamut from groovy to snooty.

## Best Local Markets

**Bondi Markets** Great people-watching and an interesting mix of goods. (p132)

**Surry Hills Markets** Very much a local affair, but only held monthly. (p108)

## Best for Food

**Eveleigh Farmers Market** The city's top foodie market, with top-quality snacks and fancy produce. (p84)

**The Rocks Market** On Fridays there are less tacky souvenirs and more tasty nosh. (p38)

**Fitzroy Gardens** This Kings Cross park has an organic food market on Saturday mornings. (p117)

## Best for Quality Goods

**Eveleigh Artisans Market** Local artisans and designers flog their wares. (p92)

**Paddington Markets** Brave the crowds to hunt out good-quality art and craft. (p111)

## Best for Cheap Stuff

**Paddy's Markets** Forget high fashion, head here for bargains and bustle. (p63)

**Glebe Markets** A more hippyish vibe; good for secondhand clothes. (p91)

## Sydney Airport

➡ The majority of visitors to Sydney arrive at **Kingsford Smith Airport**, 10km south of the city centre.

➡ Allow $50 for a taxi to Circular Quay.

➡ Airport shuttles head to hotels and hostels in the city centre, and some reach surrounding suburbs and beach destinations. Operators include **Sydney Airporter** (☎9666 9988; www.kst.com.au; adult/child $14/11), **Super Shuttle** (☎9697 2322; www .signaturelimousinessydney .com.au; airport hotels $6) and **Manly Express** (☎8065 9524; www.manlyexpress.com .au; to Manly $35).

➡ **AirportLink** (☎8337 8417; www.airportlink.com.au; to city $17; ☉5am-midnight) runs trains from both the domestic and international terminals, connecting into the main train network. They're frequent (every 10 minutes), easy to use and quick (13 minutes to Central station), but airport tickets are charged at a hefty premium.

➡ The cheapest (albeit slowest) option to Bondi Junction is bus 400 ($4.50, 1¼ hours).

# Getting Around

Sydneysiders love to complain about their public transport system, but visitors should find it easy to navigate. The train system is the lynchpin, with lines radiating out from Central station.

## Train

☑ **Best for...** Getting to Circular Quay, the city centre, Newtown, Surry Hills, Darlinghurst, Kings Cross and Bondi Junction.

➡ Sydney has a large suburban railway web with relatively frequent services.

➡ Lines don't extend to Balmain, Glebe or the Northern or Eastern Beaches.

➡ Trains run from around 5am to 1am.

➡ A short inner-city one-way trip costs $3.40.

➡ On weekends and after 9am weekdays you can buy an off-peak return ticket for not much more than a standard one-way fare.

## Bus

☑ **Best for...** Short journeys, and all the places the train doesn't go, especially the Eastern Beaches.

➡ Fares depend upon the number of 'sections' you traverse; tickets range from $2.10 to $4.50.

➡ Discount passes will save you some bucks and are handy for 'prepay only' services.

➡ Regular buses run between 5am and midnight, when Nightrider buses take over.

➡ Bus routes starting with an X indicate limited-stop express routes; those with an L have limited stops.

➡ During peak hour, buses get crowded and sometimes fail to pick up passengers at major stops if they're full.

➡ Pay the driver as you enter (correct change minimises annoyance), or dunk prepaid tickets in the green ticket machines.

➡ Increasing numbers of services are 'prepay only'.

➡ Tickets can also be purchased at numerous newsagents, corner stores and supermarkets throughout the city.

➡ If you'll be catching buses a lot (but not trains or ferries), consider a prepaid 10-ride TravelTen ticket (sections 1-2/3-5/6+ $17/28/36).

## Boat
☑ **Best for...** Taronga Zoo, Balmain, Cockatoo Island, Watsons Bay and Manly.

➡ Most Sydney ferries operate between 6am and midnight.

➡ All ferries depart from Circular Quay.

➡ The standard single fare for most harbour destinations is $5.60; boats to Manly, Sydney Olympic Park and Parramatta cost $7.

➡ If you're staying near a ferry wharf and don't think you'll be using buses or trains much, consider a prepaid 10-ride MyFerryTen ticket ($44.80).

➡ Water taxis are a fast way to shunt around the harbour (Circular Quay to Watsons Bay in as little as 15 minutes). Companies will quote on any pick-up point within the harbour

and the river, including private jetties, islands and other boats.

## Metro Light Rail (MLR)
☑ **Best for...** Pyrmont & Glebe

➡ Metro Light Rail heads from Central to Lilyfield (via Chinatown, Darling Harbour, Pyrmont and Glebe) every 10 to 15 minutes from 6am to 11pm.

➡ There's a 24-hour service from Central to The Star, with late-night trains every 30 minutes.

## Tickets & Passes
All of the state's public and many of its private services are gathered together under the umbrella of the **NSW Transport Infoline** (📞13 15 00; www.131500.com.au). The website has an excellent journey planner, where you can plug in your requirements and then let the system spit out a range of options. **MyMulti** passes allow unlimited travel on trains (except the airport stations), light rail, buses and government ferry services.

**MyMulti DayPass** ($21) Covers the entire system.

**MyMulti1** (week/month $43/164) This pass is the best option for most travellers. Includes all buses, light rail and ferries but only Zone 1 trains. (Note, you can get to Parramatta and Olympic Park on this pass by ferry but not by train.)

**MyMulti2** (week/month $51/194) As above, but includes trains to places such as Olympic Park and Parramatta.

**MyMulti3** (week/month $60/232) As above, but includes trains to Cronulla, the Blue Mountains and stations on the fringes of Royal National Park.

**Family Funday Sunday** If you're related and have at least one adult and one child in your party, all of you can travel anywhere within the network on Sundays for a day rate of $2.50 per person.

### Taxi

☑ **Best for...** Short trips around town.

➡ Taxis are easy to flag down in the city and the inner suburbs.

➡ Taxis are metered and drivers won't usually rip you off – but don't expect them to know how to get to where you're going! If they're unsure, ask them to turn off the meter while they check the map.

➡ Flagfall is $3.40; the metered fare thereafter is $2.06 per kilometre.

➡ There's a 20% surcharge between 10pm and 6am, and additional charges for tolls and radio bookings ($2.30).

➡ For more on Sydney's taxis, see www.nswtaxi .org.au.

### Reliable Operators

**Legion Cabs** (☎13 14 51; www.legioncabs.com.au)

**Premier Cabs** (☎13 10 17; www.premiercabs.com.au)

**RSL Cabs** (☎9581 1111; www.rslcabs.com.au)

**Taxis Combined** (☎13 33 00; www.taxiscombined .com.au)

### Car & Motorcycle

☑ **Best for...** Getting to the beaches quickly.

➡ Avoid driving in central Sydney if you can: there's a confusing one-way street system, parking sucks (even at hotels), and parking inspectors and tow-away zones proliferate.

➡ Conversely, a car is handy for accessing Sydney's outer reaches (particularly the beaches) and for day trips.

➡ For 24-hour emergency roadside assistance, maps, travel advice, insurance and accommodation discounts, contact the **National Roads & Motorists Association** (NRMA; ☎13 21 32; www .nrma.com.au; 74 King St; ◷9am-5pm Mon-Fri, 9.30am-12.30pm Sat; ☒Wynyard). It has reciprocal arrangements with similar organisations interstate and overseas (bring proof of membership).

### Driving

➡ Australians drive on the left-hand side of the road.

➡ The minimum driving age is 18.

➡ Overseas visitors can drive with their domestic driving licences for up to three months but must obtain a NSW driving licence after that.

➡ Speed limits in Sydney are generally 60km/h (50km/h in some areas), rising to 100km/h or 110km/h on motorways.

➡ Seat belts are compulsory; using handheld mobile phones is prohibited.

➡ A blood-alcohol limit of 0.05% is enforced with random breath tests and hefty punishments. If you're in an accident (even if you didn't cause it) and you're over the alcohol limit, your insurance will be invalidated.

### Parking

➡ Sydney's private car parks are expensive (around $15 per hour); public car parks are more affordable (sometimes under $10 per hour).

➡ The city centre and Darling Harbour have the greatest number of private car parks, but these are also the priciest.

➡ Street parking meters devour coins (from $2.50 to $5 per hour) and some take credit cards.

**Toll Roads**

➡ Sydney's motorways are all tolled; charges vary with the distance travelled – anywhere from $2 to $15.

➡ Most toll roads are cashless; hire-car companies can provide information on setting up a temporary electronic pass.

**Hire**

➡ Car rental prices vary depending on season and demand.

➡ Read the small print to check age restrictions, exactly what your insurance covers and where you can take the car (dirt roads are sometimes off limits).

➡ The big players have airport desks and city offices (mostly around William St).

➡ For motorbike hire, try Bikescape (p166).

**Bicycle**

☑ **Best for...** Keeping fit and seeing stuff.

➡ Sydney traffic can be intimidating but there are an increasing number of dedicated separate bike lanes; see www.cityofsydney.nsw .gov.au.

➡ Bike helmets are compulsory.

➡ There's no charge for taking a bike on CityRail trains, except during peak hours (6am to 9am and 3.30pm to 7.30pm Monday to Friday) when you will need to purchase a child's ticket for the bike.

➡ Bikes travel for free on Sydney's ferries, which usually have bicycle racks (first come, first served).

➡ Buses are no-go zones for bikes.

# Essential Information

**Business Hours**

Reviews in this book won't list opening hours unless they significantly differ from the standard opening hours listed here.

➡ **Restaurants** noon-3pm & 6-10pm

➡ **Cafes** 8am-4pm

➡ **Pubs** 11am-midnight Mon-Sat, 11am-10pm Sun

➡ **Shops** 9.30am-6pm Mon-Wed, Fri & Sat, 9.30am-8pm Thu, 11am-5pm Sun

➡ **Banks** 9.30am-4pm Mon-Thu, 9.30am-5pm Fri

**Discount Cards**

➡ **See Sydney & Beyond Card** (☎1300 366 476; www.seesydney card.com; 2-/3-/7-day $155/189/270, with transport $190/245/339) offers admission to a plethora of Sydney attractions, including sightseeing tours, harbour cruises, museums, historic buildings and wildlife parks. It's reasonably pricy, so assess how many of these attractions you think you'll actually visit in the timeframe before purchasing. The 'with transport' option includes a MyMulti public transport pass.

➡ **Ticket Through Time** (☎8239 2211; www .hht.net.au/visiting /ticket_through_time; adult/ concession & child $30/15) provides entry to the 11 Sydney museums of the Historic Houses Trust (HHT) for a three-month period. Tickets can be purchased online or at any HHT property.

## Electricity

240V/50Hz

## Emergency
Call ☎000 for police, ambulance or fire brigade.

## Money
☑ **Top Tip** Travellers cheques are something of a dinosaur these days, and they won't be accepted everywhere. It's easier not to bother with them.

➡ The unit of currency is the Australian dollar, which is divided into 100 cents.

➡ Notes are colourful, plastic and washing-machine-proof, in denominations of $100, $50, $20, $10 and $5.

➡ Coins come in $2, $1, 50c, 20c, 10c and 5c. The old 2c and 1c coins have been out of circulation for years, so shops round prices up (or down) to the nearest 5c. Curiously, $2 coins are smaller than $1.

### ATMs
➡ Central Sydney is chock-full of banks with 24-hour ATMs that will accept debit and credit cards linked to international network systems (Cirrus, Maestro, Visa, MasterCard etc).

➡ Most banks place a $1000 limit on the amount you can withdraw daily.

➡ You'll also find ATMs in pubs and clubs, although these usually charge slightly higher fees.

➡ Shops and retail outlets usually have Eftpos facilities, which allow you to pay for purchases with your debit or credit card.

### Credit Cards
➡ Visa and MasterCard are widely accepted at larger shops, restaurants and hotels, but not necessarily at smaller shops or cafes.

➡ Diners Club and American Express are less widely accepted.

### Money Changers
➡ Exchange bureaux are dotted around the city centre, Kings Cross and Bondi.

➡ Shop around as rates vary and most outlets charge some sort of commission.

➡ The counters at the airport are open until the last flight comes in; rates here aren't quite as good as they are in the city.

### Tipping
In Sydney, most services don't expect a tip, so you shouldn't feel pressured into giving one. If the service is good, however, it is customary to tip wait staff in restaurants (up to 10%) and taxi drivers (round up to the nearest dollar).

## Public Holidays
☑ **Top Tip** Most public holidays cleverly morph into long weekends (three days), so if a holiday such as New Year's Day falls on a weekend, the following Monday is usually a holiday.

On public holidays, government departments, banks, offices and post offices shut up shop. On Good Friday, Easter Sunday, Anzac Day and Christmas Day, most

## Money-Saving Tips

➡ While there's no such thing as a free lunch at Sydney's fine-dining restaurants, you can save a pretty penny at some of them if you know when to go. Marque in Surry Hills offers set three-course Friday lunches that are half the price you'll pay for the regular menu. Guillaume and Aria, the two closest restaurants to the Opera House, both offer cheaper pre-theatre menus.

➡ For views, put on your glad rags and zip up to Blu Bar on the 36th floor of the Shangri-La hotel or Orbit on the 47th floor of the Australia Square tower (Orbit has the advantage of rotating). They're not cheap bars but a cocktail will cost less than the price of visiting Sydney Tower.

➡ Rather than booking an expensive harbour cruise, grab a ferry to Manly to explore the outer harbour and a Parramatta river service to head upstream.

shops are closed. Public holidays include the following:

**New Year's Day** 1 January

**Australia Day** 26 January

**Easter** (Good Friday to Easter Monday) March/April

**Anzac Day** 25 April

**Queen's Birthday** Second Monday in June

**Bank Holiday** First Monday in August (only banks are closed)

**Labour Day** First Monday in October

**Christmas Day** 25 December

**Boxing Day** 26 December

Something else to consider when planning a Sydney visit is school holidays, when accommodation rates soar and everything gets decidedly hectic. Sydney students have a long summer break that includes Christmas and most of January. Other school holidays fall around March to April (Easter), late June to mid-July, and late September to early October.

## Telephone

☑ **Top Tip** Toll-free numbers start with the prefix ☎1800, while numbers that start with ☎1300 are only the cost of a local call.

➡ Public telephones, which can be found all over the city, take phonecards, credit cards and occasionally (if the coin slots aren't jammed up) coins.

➡ Australia's country code: ☎61

➡ Sydney's area code: ☎02 (drop the zero when dialling into Australia).

➡ International access code: ☎0011 (used when dialling other countries from Australia).

**Mobile Phones**

➡ Australian mobile phone numbers have four-digit prefixes starting with ☎04.

➡ Australia's digital network is compatible with GSM 900 and 1800 handsets (used in Europe). Quad-band US phones will work, but you'll need an unlocked handset to use an Australian SIM.

## Tourist Information

☑ **Top Tip** Opening hours for information centres vary with the seasons; summer hours may be longer than those listed here.

**City Host Information Kiosks** (www.cityofsydney .nsw.gov.au) Circular Quay (cnr Pitt & Alfred Sts; ⏱9am-5pm; 🚆Circular Quay); Town Hall (George St; ⏱9am-5pm; 🚆Town Hall); Haymarket (Dixon St; ⏱11am-7pm; 🚆Town Hall)

**Manly Visitor Information Centre** (🕿9976 1430; www.manlyaustralia .com.au; Manly Wharf; ⏱9am-5pm Mon-Fri, 10am-4pm Sat & Sun; ⛴Manly) This helpful visitors centre, just outside the ferry wharf and alongside the bus interchange, has free pamphlets covering the Manly Scenic Walkway and other Manly attractions, plus loads of local bus information.

**Sydney Harbour National Park Information Centre** (🕿9253 0888; www.environment.nsw.gov.au; Cadman's Cottage, 110 George St; ⏱10am-4.30pm; Circular Quay) Has maps of walks in different parts of the park and organises tours of the harbour islands.

**Sydney Visitor Centre – Darling Harbour** (🕿9240 8788; www.darlingharbour.com; ⏱9.30am-5.30pm; 🚆Town Hall) Behind the IMAX Cinema, with bountiful info about NSW, tours, hotels and entertainment options.

**Sydney Visitor Centre – The Rocks** (🕿9240 8788; www.sydneyvisitorcentre.com; cnr Argyle & Playfair Sts; ⏱9.30am-5.30pm; 🚆Circular Quay) Sydney's main visitors centre, with walls of brochures and information on Sydney and regional NSW. Knowledgeable staff can help you find a hotel or a restaurant with harbour views, book a tour, hire a car and arrange transport for day trips out of town. Info on exploring The Rocks is the obvious specialty.

## Travellers with Disabilities

☑ **Top Tip** Some taxis accommodate wheelchairs – request them when you make your booking.

➡ Compared with many other major cities, Sydney has great access for citizens and visitors with disabilities.

➡ Most of Sydney's main attractions are accessible by wheelchair, and all new or renovated buildings must, by law, include wheelchair access. Older buildings can pose some problems, however, and some restaurants and entertainment venues aren't quite up to scratch. Most of the National Trust's historic houses are at least partially accessible.

➡ Most of Sydney's major attractions offer hearing loops and sign-language interpreters for hearing-impaired travellers. To expedite proceedings, contact venue staff in advance.

➡ Many new buildings incorporate architectural features that are helpful to the vision impaired, such as textured floor details at the top and bottom of stairs. Sydney's pedestrian crossings feature catchy beep-and-buzz sound cues.

### Organisations

**City of Sydney** (🕿9265 9333; www.cityofsydney.nsw .gov.au) Lists parking spaces, transport information, CBD access maps and other information.

**Deaf Society of NSW**
(☎9893 8555; www.deaf
societynsw.org.au)

**Roads and Traffic
Authority** (RTA; ☎13 22 13;
www.rta.nsw.gov.au) Sup-
plies temporary parking
permits for international
drivers with disabilities.

**Spinal Cord Injuries Aus-
tralia** (www.spinalcord
injuries.com.au)

**Vision Australia** (☎1300
847 466; www.vision
australia.org.au)

## Visas

☑ **Top Tip** All visitors to
Australia need a visa –
only New Zealand nation-
als are exempt, and even
they receive a 'special
category' visa on arrival.

➡ Visa application forms
are available from Australian diplomatic missions
overseas, travel agents or
the website of the **Department of Immigration &
Citizenship** (DIAC; ☎13 18
81; www.immi.gov.au).

➡ Citizens of EU member
countries, Andorra, Iceland,
Liechtenstein, Monaco,

Norway, San Marino and
Switzerland are eligible for
an **eVisitor**, which is free
and allows visitors to stay
in Australia for up to three
months. eVisitors must
be applied for online and
are electronically stored
and linked to individual
passport numbers, so no
stamp in your passport is
required. Apply at least 14
days prior to the proposed
date of travel to Australia.
Applications are made
on the Department of
Immigration & Citizenship
website.

➡ An **Electronic Travel
Authority (ETA)** allows
visitors to enter Aus-
tralia anytime within a 12
month period and stay
for up to three months
at a time (unlike eVisitor,
multiple entries are per-
mitted). Travellers from
qualifying countries can
get an ETA through any
International Air Trans-
port Association (IATA)–
registered travel agent
or overseas airline. They
make the application
for you when you buy a
ticket and issue the ETA,

which replaces the usual
visa stamped in your
passport. It's common
practice for travel agents
to charge a fee for issu-
ing an ETA (in the vicinity
of US$25). This system
is available to passport
holders of some 33 coun-
tries, including all of the
countries that are eligible
for eVisitor. The eight
countries that are eligible
for ETA but not eVisitor
(Brunei, Canada, Hong
Kong, Japan, Malaysia,
Singapore, South Korea
and the USA) can make
their application online
at www.eta.immi.gov.au,
where a $20 fee applies.

➡ If you are from a
country not covered by
eVisitor or ETA, or you
want to stay longer than
three months, you'll need
to apply for a visa. **Tourist visas** cost $110 and
allow single or multiple
entry for stays of three,
six or twelve months and
are valid for use within 12
months of issue.

# Index

See also separate subindexes for:

Eating p187
Drinking p188
Entertainment p189
Shopping p189



**Sights p000**
Map Pages **p000**

Sights p000
Map Pages **p000**

# Behind the Scenes

## Send Us Your Feedback

We love to hear from travellers – your comments help make our books better. We read every word, and we guarantee that your feedback goes straight to the authors. Visit **lonelyplanet.com/contact** to submit your updates and suggestions.

Note: We may edit, reproduce and incorporate your comments in Lonely Planet products such as guidebooks, websites and digital products, so let us know if you don't want your comments reproduced or your name acknowledged. For a copy of our privacy policy visit lonelyplanet.com/privacy.

## Peter's Thanks

Special thanks to David Mills, Barry Sawtell, Michael Woodhouse, Tim Moyes and especially Tony Dragicevich and Debbie Debono. Thanks also to Shenita Prasad, Shelley Mulhern, Jo Brook, Sue Ostler, John Burfitt, Braith Bamkin, Daniel Dragicevich, Lauren Dragicevich and Matt Dragicevich for on-the-road advice and company.

## Acknowledgments

Cover photograph: Sydney Opera House and Harbour Bridge; John Banagan/Getty Images ©.

Top Sights p9: Art Gallery of NSW, John Kaldor Family Gallery. Installation view of John Kaldor Family Gallery © Richard Long, *Spring showers circle*, 1992 (foreground), © Gilbert & George, DIG, 2005, © Richard Long, *Southern Gravity*, 1992.

## This Book

This 3rd edition of Lonely Planet's *Pocket Sydney* guidebook was researched and written by Peter Dragicevich. The previous two editions were written by Charles Rawlings-Way. This guidebook was commissioned in Lonely Planet's Melbourne office, and produced by the following:

**Commissioning Editor** Maryanne Netto

**Coordinating Editors** Alison Ridgway, Gabrielle Stefanos **Coordinating Cartographer** Rachel Imeson **Coordinating Layout Designer** Adrian Blackburn **Managing Editors** Barbara Delissen, Martine Power **Senior Editor** Susan Paterson **Managing Cartographers** Anita Bahn, David Connolly, Mark Griffiths **Managing Layout Designer** Jane Hart **Assisting Editors** Kate Morgan, Amanda Williamson

**Cover Research** Naomi Parker **Internal Image Research** Claire Gibson, Aude Vauconsant

**Thanks to** Liz Abbott, Dan Austin, Laura Crawford, Ryan Evans, Tobias Gattineau, Chris Girdler, Jouve India, Asha Ioculari, Andi Jones, Ali Lemer, Trent Paton, Molly Roberts, Averil Robertson, Dianne Schallmeiner, Suzannah Shwer, Amanda Sierp, Fiona Siseman, Sophie Splatt, Gerard Walker

# Our Writer

### Peter Dragicevich

After a decade of frequent flights between his native New Zealand and Sydney, the bright lights and endless beach days drew Peter across the Tasman on a more permanent basis. For the best part of the next decade he would call Sydney's inner suburbs home, while managing the city's most popular gay and lesbian newspaper, followed by a stable of upmarket food, fashion and photography magazines. More recently he's coauthored dozens of books for Lonely Planet, including the *Sydney* city guide and four other Australian titles.

**Published by Lonely Planet Publications Pty Ltd**
ABN 36 005 607 983
3rd edition – Dec 2012
ISBN 978 1 74179 820 3
© Lonely Planet 2012  Photographs © as indicated 2012
10 9 8 7 6 5 4 3 2 1
Printed in China